GOD HAS A PLAN FOR

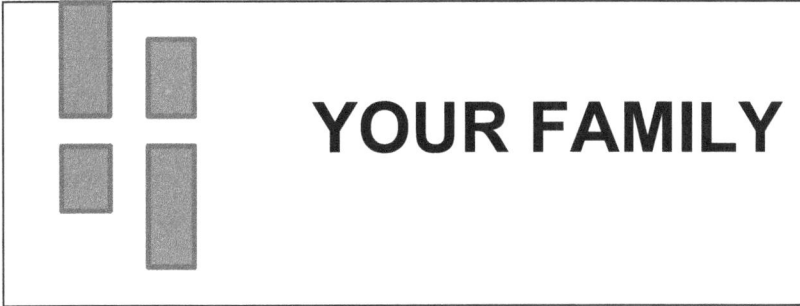

YOUR FAMILY

FAMILY GOVERNMENT

For I know the plans I have for you," declares the LORD, "plans to prosper you and not to harm you, plans to give you hope and a future.
Jeremiah 29:11

By David Lange

GOD HAS A PLAN FOR YOUR FAMILY
FAMILY GOVERNMENT
By David E. Lange

Published by Lange Publishing, Pacific, MO
Library of Congress Control Number: 2014911673
ISBN 978-0-9824070-3-5
ISBN 0-9824070-3-3
Printed in the United States of America

This book is dedicated to . . .

Christy. She is my wonderful, supportive, and beautiful wife. Without the support of her and my awesome kids, Jeremiah, Bethany, Sofia, Bentley, and Blake this work would not have been possible.

Dad and Mom. I cherish the godly parents that I have been blessed with.

Mission Community Church. I also want to acknowledge and thank our church family for putting up with me during this process.

Debra. My very supportive sister, her family, Jon Marc, Nathan, Micah, and Natalie.

Of course the greatest honor and glory goes to Jesus Christ, my Lord and Savior!

For more information check out
WWW.BIBLEISTHEROCK.COM

If you were blessed by this series check out
WWW.FIVECOMMITMENTS.COM

CONTENTS

MUST READ INTRODUCTION: GOD HAS A PLAN

God loves you. He created you. He longs for you to get to know Him better and to walk in His ways. God's love includes a plan for you, your family, the church, and the nation. He fully describes His plan in the Bible.

God's Word warns us about consequences that will occur when a nation turns away from Him. How do you think America is doing? Are we better off today? Are we worse off? The evidence is clear. We are experiencing some of God's consequences right now.

CONSEQUENCES FOR TURNING AWAY FROM GOD AND HIS WORD

- Debt - Deuteronomy 28:44
- More natural disasters –
  Deuteronomy 28:22-24; 2 Chronicles 7:13
- Losing God's protection –
  Deuteronomy 28:25
- A far away nation whose language we do not understand will come against us -
  Deuteronomy 28:49-50

President Andrew Jackson said, ***"The Bible is the rock on which our republic rests."*** This was true when our nation began, but it is no longer true today.

Today we have removed prayer, the Ten Commandments, and the Bible from our schools. Our families no longer devote time to studying Scripture and to following God's truths and principles.

People believe the lie that the founders wanted a separation of church and state. This lie distorts the meaning of the first amendment. It claims that having God in our schools breaks this amendment. But if this was true, would the authors and founders of the first amendment have had the Bible as the main textbook in their public schools? For four centuries, American families have cherished the Bible. They have believed it to be the rock on which this republic should rest.

In 1647, the first law for public education in America was called, "The Old Deluder Satan Act." The law declared, *"It being one chief project of that old deluder, Satan, to keep men from the knowledge of the Scriptures, as in former time…* Satan's goal is to keep men from the Holy Scriptures because God's Word is what leads people to a saving faith in Christ. Teaching Christianity is the best safeguard for any nation. To remove the teachings of Christ and His Word is to destroy a nation.

Societies of men must be governed in one way or another. They can either be governed with a heavy hand from a civil government or they can be self-governed based upon the teachings of Christ.

Heavy-handed government cannot restrain the sinfulness of man. Christ and Christ alone can change the character of man.

The foundation of Christ and His Word is what keeps a nation free. Do you think our nation is better off after removing God from our public schools? Are we less greedy, violent, or depressed? Are we more financially stable? Are our families more unified and loving or more separated and torn apart? America is suffering because we have taken God out of our lives. We need to repent and accept His perfect plan today.

Our country doesn't have to be this way. We can change the direction of this nation if we repent. Our founders knew this. They stood up and made a declaration to the world that they believed in a Creator. They understood that God had given them unalienable rights to be free and to worship Him as they pleased.

Do you believe the same? Are you willing to stand up for what you believe? Are you willing to cherish the Bible and begin studying it to find out what God's plan is for you, your family, the church, and our nation?

The four books in this series cover God's four ordained institutions: Self-Government / Family Government / Church Government / Civil Government.

They describe ten Life Truths for each institution. Each chapter presents a different Life Truth; a foundation for returning to God and for putting Him and His Word first in your life. Make a commitment to memorize these Life Truths as you work through the chapters.

CONSENT OF THE GOVERNED – ONE FAMILY AT A TIME

Our republic is still based upon the consent of the people. We are a government of the people, by the people, and for the people. As you return to God, and begin fulfilling the purposes God has for you in each of these institutions, seek to recruit others. Pray for our nation. Reach out to others in the hope that God will open their eyes and see the importance of obeying Him.

GOALS TO PRAY FOR:

- Individuals and families to return to studying, memorizing, and obeying God's Word
- Public schools to make the Bible the main textbook again
- The Ten Commandments to be obeyed and taught in our nation

ENGAGE PEOPLE WITH QUESTIONS LIKE THESE:

- Do you know that God has a plan for you, your family, the church, and our nation?
- Do you think our nation is headed in the right direction?
- Do you think our nation is more violent? More greedy?
- Do you think it was a good idea that we removed God and the Ten Commandments from our schools?
- Do you know God's Word says there will be consequences if we turn away from Him? *(Debt, loss of His protection, attacks from a nation from far away whose language we do not understand, more natural disasters)*
- Do you know that God will bless us if we turn back to Him?

FOLLOW UP WITH THIS QUESTION:

- Would you be interested in a Bible Study to learn more about God's plan for you, your family, the church, and our nation?

God allows suffering when we choose to turn away from Him. God promises blessings when we return to Him. Let's return to God and encourage everyone to do the same.

A PLAN OF ACTION FOR YOU, YOUR FAMILY, AND YOUR COMMUNITY:

1. Study and memorize the Life Truths for each institution.
2. Encourage others to join you (door to door, work, family, newspaper, etc…)
3. Encourage others to pray about running for a public office (school board, superintendent, alderman, mayor, etc…)
4. Begin a Facebook page or any other type of social media that will keep people informed (Have your goals clearly marked: We believe in God, the Apostles Creed, the Bible as the rock on which this nation rests, etc…) –This will help alert people to show up at City Hall for a vote or to voice their opinions.
5. Vote for Biblical laws. (Ex: a return to teaching the Bible in public schools)
6. **Direct people to the website *www.bibleistherock.com* for more information.**

A CHALLENGE FOR TODAY

Our founders understood the importance of knowing and heeding God's Word for future posterity. They also understood that godly leaders would need to be trained in the Bible. The first schools in our nation made sure that students got a Biblical education so they could lead with God's Word being the source for all law.

If we are going to have godly laws that lead us in righteousness, then we are going to need men and women who are willing to be the lawmakers. Who do we want in office making the laws that govern our nation? **Men and women who are God-fearing and who know the Bible well.**

For this to happen, "Christian" schools must make it a priority in their curriculum to raise up such leaders and prepare them for public offices. Not only do our "Christian" schools need to step up and refocus some of their goals, but we as a people need to engage more on a local level. We need to be willing to serve as mayors, aldermen, superintendents, and local school board members.

We must return to God so that He can forgive our sin and heal our land. We need to have a confidence and boldness to speak up for what we believe in. We need to study God's Word and teach all who will listen.

If we pray, study God's Word, obey Him, and spread the gospel, then we will be blessed by Him. God will hear our prayers, forgive our sins, and heal America again.

This is not an exhaustive study on the institutions just a starter guide to help us get things back into God's perfect order. *"His will being done on earth as it is in heaven."*

Read all four books and learn God's plan for the institutions.

Book 1 *God has a plan for you*
Self-Government

Book 2 *God has a plan for your family*
Family Government

Book 3 *God has a plan for the church*
Church Government

Book 4 *God has a plan for our nation*
Civil Government

**May God bless you and
may God bless our nation!**

TEN FAMILY GOVERNMENT LIFE TRUTHS

I. THE FAMILY IS GOD'S DESIGN

Question: What is God's design for a family?
Answer: God's design for a family is one man, one woman and their children.

Mark 10:6-8 (NIV) [6] "But at the beginning of creation God 'made them male and female.' [7] 'For this reason a man will leave his father and mother and be united to his wife, [8] and the two will become one flesh.' So they are no longer two, but one.

2. A FATHER'S RESPONSIBILITIES

Question: What is God's design for a father?
Answer: God's design for a father is to lead his family, love his wife, and bring his children up in the training and instruction of the Lord.

Ephesians 6:4 (NIV) [4] Fathers, do not exasperate your children; instead, bring them up in the training and instruction of the Lord.

3. A MOTHER'S RESPONSIBILITIES

Question: What is God's design for a mother?

Answer: God's design for a mother is to empower her husband to lead, manage the home, and help raise the righteous.

Titus 2:3-5 (NIV) ³ Likewise, teach the older women to be reverent in the way they live, not to be slanderers or addicted to much wine, but to teach what is good. ⁴ Then they can train the younger women to love their husbands and children, ⁵ to be self-controlled and pure, to be busy at home, to be kind, and to be subject to their husbands, so that no one will malign the word of God.

4. CHILDREN'S RESPONSIBILITIES

Question: What is God's design for children?
Answer: God's design for a child is to know Christ, obey authority and grow up to lead in society.

Ephesians 6:1-3 (NIV) ¹ Children, obey your parents in the Lord, for this is right. ² "Honor your father and mother"– which is the first commandment with a promise– ³ "that it may go well with you and that you may enjoy long life on the earth."

5. THE FAMILY IS RESPONSIBLE TO GET RID OF ANGER

Question: What are we to do with anger?
Answer: Our responsibility is to get rid of man's anger and be kind to one another.

Ephesians 4:31-32 (NIV) ^{31} *Get rid of all bitterness, rage and anger, brawling and slander, along with every form of malice.* ^{32} *Be kind and compassionate to one another, forgiving each other, just as in Christ God forgave you.*

6. THE FAMILY IS RESPONSIBLE TO HAVE AN ALTAR

Question: Where should we go when dissension and disunity arise in our family?
Answer: Our responsibility is to come to the altar and heal the issues in our family?

Numbers 6:24-27 (NIV) ^{24} *"' "The LORD bless you and keep you;* ^{25} *the LORD make his face shine upon you and be gracious to you;* ^{26} *the LORD turn his face toward you and give you peace."'* ^{27} *"So they will put my name on the Israelites, and I will bless them."*

7. THE FAMILY IS RESPONSIBLE TO TEACH DISCIPLINE

Question: What should we do when our home is getting out of order?
Answer: Our responsibility is to discipline ourselves to fulfill God's purposes.

Hebrews 12:11 (NIV) ^{11} *No discipline seems pleasant at the time, but painful. Later on, however, it produces a harvest of righteousness and peace for those who have been trained by it.*

8. THE FAMILY IS RESPONSIBLE TO TEACH FINANCES

Question: How should Christians view debt?
Answer: Christians should do all they can to get out of and stay out of debt.

Proverbs 22:7 (NIV) [7] The rich rule over the poor, and the borrower is servant to the lender.

9. THE FAMILY IS RESPONSIBLE TO PRACTICE HOSPITALITY

Question: How should Christians view their homes?
Answer: Christians should use their homes as ministry centers.

Romans 12:13 (NIV) [13] Share with God's people who are in need. Practice hospitality.

10. THE FAMILY IS RESPONSIBLE FOR HEALTHCARE

Question: How should Christians view the needy?
Answer: Christians should provide for those in need, especially in their immediate family.

1 Timothy 5:8 (NIV) [8] If anyone does not provide for his relatives, and especially for his immediate family, he has denied the faith and is worse than an unbeliever.

FAMILY-GOVERNMENT
LIFE TRUTH # 1
THE FAMILY IS GOD'S DESIGN

Family government is the second institution that God designed. First, he created man and gave us responsibilities that we are to fulfill as we discussed in Self Government. After man was created then God created woman and established the family. *Genesis 2:18-24 (NIV) [18] The LORD God said, "It is not good for the man to be alone. I will make a helper suitable for him." [19] Now the LORD God had formed out of the ground all the beasts of the field and all the birds of the air. He brought them to the man to see what he would name them; and whatever the man called each living creature, that was its name. [20] So the man gave names to all the livestock, the birds of the air and all the beasts of the field. But for Adam no suitable helper was found. [21] So the LORD God caused the man to fall into a deep sleep; and while he was sleeping, he took one of the man's ribs and closed up the place with flesh. [22] Then the LORD God made a woman from the rib he had taken out of the man, and he brought her to the man. [23] The man said, "This is now bone of my bones and flesh of my flesh; she shall be called 'woman,' for she was taken out of man." [24] For this reason a man will leave his father and mother and be united to his wife, and they will become one flesh.*

The family has responsibilities to obey just as we do for Self Government. Jesus reinstated this institution in the New Testament when He said in, *Mark 10:6-9*

(NIV) ⁶ "But at the beginning of creation God 'made them male and female.' ⁷ 'For this reason a man will leave his father and mother and be united to his wife, ⁸ and the two will become one flesh.' So they are no longer two, but one. ⁹ Therefore what God has joined together, let man not separate."

Jesus reminded us that this was God's intent from the very beginning of creation. God's plan for our lives is always best and his perfect plan for a family is to be a man, a woman and their children. Notice the family that God instituted is not a man and a man or a woman and a woman, but it is one man and one woman. Throughout history people have sought to change God's design and through their disobedience curses from God have come. God blesses us for our obedience to His stipulations.

Part of the revival that America needs is a return to the importance of the God designed family. As we return to God and obey His stipulations God will again bless our nation. Just before the great flood God saw how corrupt and violent man had become because man had turned away from God's law.

It says in, *Genesis 6:12 (NIV) ¹² God saw how corrupt the earth had become, for all the people on earth had corrupted their ways.* When we decide to disobey God's law we corrupt our ways and consequences will follow. Society will become more violent and perverted.

It is vital to the restoration of our nation for us to return to God's stipulations and obey them as Noah did. *Genesis 7:5 (NIV) ⁵ And Noah did all that the LORD commanded him.* God's provisions, blessings, and protection are tied to our obedience. When the flood came Noah was protected as it says in, *Genesis 7:1 (NIV) ¹ The LORD then said to Noah, "Go into the ark, you and your whole family, because I have found you righteous in this generation.*

As we learn God's rules for family government let us be the ones who repent and hear God say of us, "I have found you righteous in this generation."

We will look at the three God given responsibilities for the family.

1. The family is to procreate

God's design for a family is for them to be fruitful and fill the earth.

Genesis 1:27-28 (NIV) ²⁷ So God created man in his own image, in the image of God he created him; male and female he created them. ²⁸ God blessed them and said to them, "Be fruitful and increase in number; fill the earth and subdue it. Rule over the fish of the sea and the birds of the air and over every living creature that moves on the ground." When a man and a woman come together in marriage one of their main responsibilities is to have children. This has been the intent of the family since the beginning. This is just one reason why a man and a man or a woman and a woman are not meant to be the leaders in a family. They cannot procreate.

God is the creator of all and he chooses for us to be a small part of the creation process. The command to procreate comes with blessings and curses. When we are obeying God He makes more children through us and the nation of the righteous grows and is powerful. *Deuteronomy 28:1-4 (NIV) ¹ If you fully obey the LORD your God and carefully follow all his commands I give you today, the LORD your God will set you high above all the nations on earth. ² All these blessings will come upon you and accompany you if you obey the LORD your God: ³ You will be blessed in the city and blessed in the country. ⁴ **The fruit of your womb will be blessed**, and the crops of your land and the young of your livestock–the calves of your herds and the lambs of your flocks.*

When we disobey God He causes the fruit of the womb to be cursed. He then will allow another nation to multiply among us and place us into slavery. *Deuteronomy 28:18 (NIV) ¹⁸ **The fruit of your womb will be cursed,** and the crops of your land, and the calves of your herds and the lambs of your flocks. Deuteronomy 28:43 (NIV) ⁴³ The alien who lives among you will rise above you higher and higher, but you will sink lower and lower.*

There are times in history when God chose not to give a family a child until later in their life. The Bible calls this term being barren. Sarai, Rebekah, Rachel, and Elizabeth all dealt with barrenness and had a child later in life. Children are a blessing from God and He decides when and to whom we will be born.

God's plan for everyone is not that they be married. Some will remain single, some will be widowed, and many will be married.

All of us came from a family and we need to learn and teach others God's design for the family. We all have people we can influence toward righteousness. Obedience equals fruitful wombs. Look at this promise for Israel if they will be obedient to God's commands. *Deuteronomy 7:14 (NIV) [14] You will be blessed more than any other people; none of your men or women will be childless, nor any of your livestock without young.*

Our responsibility as a godly family is to be fruitful and fill the earth with God fearing people. In our generation many people see children as a problem or an inconvenience, but God sees them as a blessing. When we see a large family we may look down upon them and think that they are crazy for having so many children. The Bible calls a family who has many children blessed. *Psalm 127:3-5 (NIV) [3] Sons are a heritage from the LORD, children a reward from him. [4] Like arrows in the hands of a warrior are sons born in one's youth. [5] Blessed is the man whose quiver is full of them. They will not be put to shame when they contend with their enemies in the gate.*
Proverbs 17:6 (NIV) [6] Children's children are a crown to the aged, and parents are the pride of their children.

In our self-centered society we do not want to serve others and raise children. We want to be entertained, comfortable, and blessed. God's design is that we have godly families who train children to know Him and lead in society. We are created to serve God and fulfill his purposes.

2. The family is to raise up the righteous.

God has given to us the principles for a free and prosperous nation. Any nation who will make Jesus the Lord, submit to the Ten Commandments, and follow the teachings of Christ will be blessed. *Psalm 33:12 (NIV)* [12] *Blessed is the nation whose God is the LORD, the people he chose for his inheritance.*

Throughout history we have seen this to be true and we have especially seen the power of this truth in America. America has been the most blessed nation of all and it is because we founded this nation upon God and His principles.

One of the first things that our Congress printed was the Aitken Bible. The Aitken Bible was endorsed and printed by Congress and distributed to the schools and families of this nation. It was called, "The Bible of the Revolution."

THE

HOLY BIBLE,

Containing the OLD and NEW

TESTAMENTS:

Newly tranflated out of the

ORIGINAL TONGUES;

And with the former

TRANSLATIONS

Diligently compared and revifed.

PHILADELPHIA:
PRINTED AND SOLD BY R. AITKEN, AT POPE'S
HEAD, THREE DOORS ABOVE THE COFFEE
HOUSE, IN MARKET STREET.
M,DCC,LXXXII.

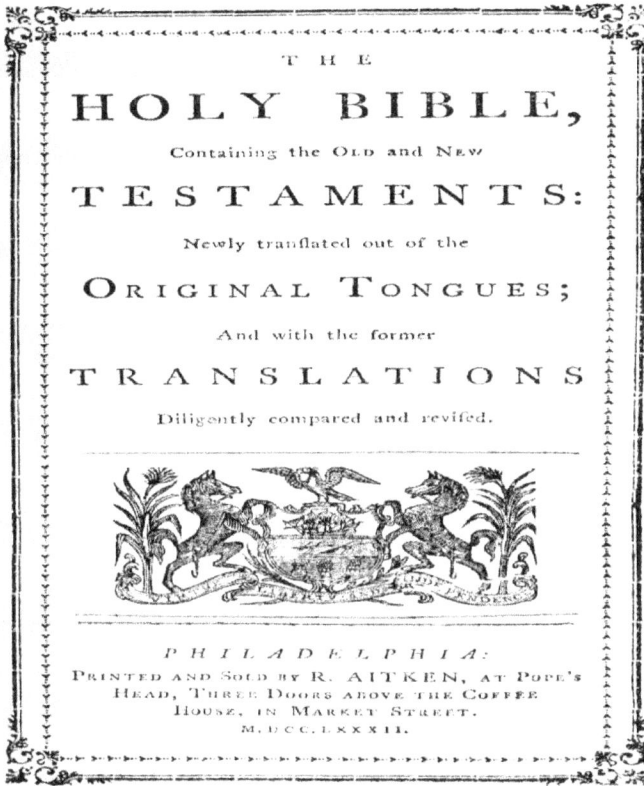

Our founders, congress included, new that for us to be a free and prosperous nation we would need to raise Godly children who knew God's Word and applied it to their lives. A nation is blessed when the Righteous rule. If we have God fearing leaders who are self-governed according to God's Word then we have an awesome nation that will be blessed by God. When we have the ungodly ruling, decisions will be made that will affect everyone and cause us to go into slavery. It says in *Proverbs 29:2 (NIV)* [2] *When the righteous thrive, the people rejoice; when the wicked rule, the people groan.*

How can we get the godly to rule? What is God's plan for the godly being in office? God's plan is for the family to raise up righteous leaders who can disciple the nations. When the family fails to fulfill its purpose the nation suffers.

When the family begins to fail then the government tends to try and fill the gap. The government has become more and more powerful in the last 100 years. Each year they continue to rule in areas that are not in God's design for the government.
Dr. James Dobson says, "The greatest tragedy of the 20th century was the breakdown of the family in the west." In 1960 6% of children were born without fathers. Today over 40% of children are born without fathers.

In the 1800's 4% of marriages ended in divorce. Today almost half of all marriages end in divorce. The statistics are the same for families in the church. About 70% of children will not grow up with a father and mother in the home for their first 18 years. God's plan is that a man and a woman come together in marriage and remain married until death do they part. The only biblical reason for divorce is marital unfaithfulness, but many today divorce because they do not want to be the servant of another. They do not want to submit to one another. Jesus said that anyone who divorces and remarries, except for marital unfaithfulness commits adultery. *Matthew 19:9 (NIV) ^{9} I tell you that anyone who divorces his wife, except*

for marital unfaithfulness, and marries another woman commits adultery."
Malachi 2:16 (NIV) [16] *"I hate divorce," says the LORD God of Israel.* As more and more families fall apart the health or our nation deteriorates.

God's design for the family is to train up godly men and women who can lead out in the principles and teachings of Christ. Leaders are to be nurtured in the family unit and then sent out to minister. Leaders are trained to forgive, serve, and minister through the issues in relationships. All relationships have issues and the righteous learn how to love one another as Christ has loved us.

Look at the qualifications for a leader in church government. *1 Timothy 3:2-5 (NIV)* [2] *Now the overseer must be above reproach,* <u>*the husband of but one wife,*</u> *temperate, self-controlled, respectable, hospitable, able to teach,* [3] *not given to drunkenness, not violent but gentle, not quarrelsome, not a lover of money.* [4] *He must manage his own family well and see that his children obey him with proper respect.* [5] ***(If anyone does not know how to manage his own family, how can he take care of God's church?)*** If the leader cannot manage his own family he should not be a leader in the church. The process for a godly nation is that we govern ourselves in the institutions and promote those who have proven themselves into higher levels of authority. If we cannot govern ourselves and our families then we are not qualified to lead in the church or the civil government.

Unfortunately, in our generation we hear people say the opposite, "Don't worry about their private life." There private life is how we are to judge if they are qualified or not to lead. If they are lying and deceiving their own family you can be sure they will lie and deceive us. A nation that has turned their back on God and His word will not care about an individual's personal life.

The Ten Commandments and the teachings of Christ are how we will raise up the righteous. There is no other way, because there is no other God. How can we be blessed by God when we turn our back on God? How can we be blessed by God when we acknowledge other religions as equals?

We used to be "One nation under God". The God is singular and we know what God they believed in by the Bible congress endorsed and printed; Jesus the God of the Holy Scriptures. On our money it still says, "In God we trust." We used to be proud to display the Ten Commandments on our Courthouses and other public buildings. People have been sworn into elected offices by placing their hands on a Bible. Why would God bless us for such actions? He would bless us because we would be obeying the first command of the Ten Commandments. *Deuteronomy 5:7 (NIV)* [7] *"You shall have no other gods before me.* When we accept all religions as valid and equal that is to go against God and His Word. *2 Samuel 7:22 (NIV)* [22] *"How great you are, O Sovereign LORD! There is no one like you, and **there is no God but you,***

Our Christian nation is not one where we will force everyone to be a Christian but we want to be following Him and His Word in order for us to be blessed. Christians have a responsibility to raise up the righteous and lead the nation into blessings. As the great commission states we are to teach the natins to obey all things that Christ taught us. Those who do not want to follow God are foolish and will experience the judgments of the Almighty. *Psalm 14:1 (NIV) ¹ The fool says in his heart, "There is no God." They are corrupt, their deeds are vile; there is no one who does good.*

Christians realize that there is only one way to God and that is through Jesus the Christ. *John 14:6 (NIV) ⁶ Jesus answered, "I am the way and the truth and the life. No one comes to the Father except through me.*

3. The family is responsible for education

With the breakdown of the family the government has taken on more and more control. One of the areas that is not the government's responsibility is in the area of education. God has given parents the responsibility to educate their children. *Deuteronomy 6:4-9 (NIV) ⁴ Hear, O Israel: The LORD our God, the LORD is one. ⁵ Love the LORD your God with all your heart and with all your soul and with all your strength. ⁶ These commandments that I give you today are to be upon your hearts. ⁷ **Impress them on your children. Talk about them when you sit at home and when*** *you walk along the road, when you lie down and when you get up. ^{8} Tie them as symbols on your hands and bind them on your foreheads. ^{9} Write them on the doorframes of your houses and on your gates.*

When we send our kids off to an institution that is godless and teaching them humanistic philosophies we will experience the fruit of their hollow philosophies. It is vital for parents to begin learning, applying, and teaching the Biblical truths to their Children.

*Hosea 4:6 (NIV) ^{6} **my people are destroyed from lack of knowledge.** "Because you have rejected knowledge, I also reject you as my priests; because you have ignored the law of your God, I also will ignore your children.*

The Civil Government has clearly stated that they no longer want the Bible to be taught in school, they no longer want prayer to be said in school, and they want us to just sit back while they choose what is best to teach our children. In our lack of knowledge of the Scriptures we have just allowed them to take prayer, the bible, and the Ten Commandments out of our schools. When this happens we will see violence and other perversions grow in our nation.

Parents we cannot just sit back and think that this is no big deal. The future of our nation depends on if we will repent and turn back to God or not. Each and every parent will be judged upon how they trained their children in the Word.

We are required by God to impress the commands of God upon our children. You will not be able to stand before God and say, "It's not my fault, I sent them to school and they did not teach them your ways."

A.A. Hodge was the first principal of Princeton Seminary in the 1800's. Even back then people were proposing a godless education. When Princeton was formed it was an institution that would educate men and women in the Word of God. Hodge said, "I am sure as I am of the fact of Christ's reign that a comprehensive and centralized system of national education separated from religion, as is now commonly proposed, will prove the most appalling enginery for the propagation of anti-Christian and atheistic unbelief, and of anti-social, nihilistic ethics, individual, social, and political, which this sin rent world has ever seen." We are seeing the effects of an education that does not begin with salvation and continue in the Word of God.

Our nation is the product of the protestant reformation and Martin Luther's teachings. Here is what Martin Luther said, *"I am afraid that schools will prove to be the great gates of hell unless they diligently labor in explaining the Holy Scriptures, engraving them in the hearts of youth. I advise no one to place his child where the Scriptures do not reign paramount. Every institution in which men are not increasingly occupied with the Word of God must become corrupt."*

My family has personally chosen to home school our children and bring them up in the training and instruction of the Lord. Some families may feel inadequate or perhaps they are a single parent and unable, but the fact of the matter is we must begin to speak up. Homeschool families and public school families we must unite on this front. We must begin to say that we want the Bible, prayer, Ten Commandments, and the teachings of Jesus back in our schools. I have begun to advocate in our community and I would encourage many to do the same in their communities.

If families begin to raise their children with this mindset and teach them the importance putting God back in schools then, as they become the next leaders in the community the laws will begin to change back to honoring God. It must start with the family educating the children in this direction and raising them up for this very purpose.

Some families may want to just hide and educate their children and not worry about the nation, but that is not the gospel we have been called to. We have been called to "teach the nations to obey all things that Christ taught." We cannot just sit back and watch the many children grow up in a godless institution being taught humanistic philosophies that will lead them straight to hell. We must speak up and say, "We want God back in our schools." We want kids to be saved and filled with a new nature in order for us to be a blessed nation.

If we just hide and do nothing many souls will be lost and our nation will perish.

Do you believe that God's Word is the only thing that should govern us? Do you believe that if we obey God's Commands He will sustain, provide, and protect us? The people who will submit to Jesus and follow His commands will be blessed.

*Deuteronomy 4:5-9 (NIV) [5] See, I have taught you decrees and laws as the LORD my God commanded me, so that you may follow them in the land you are entering to take possession of it.[6] Observe them carefully, for this will show your wisdom and understanding to the nations, who will hear about all these decrees and say, "Surely this great nation is a wise and understanding people." [7] What other nation is so great as to have their gods near them the way the LORD our God is near us whenever we pray to him? [8] And what other nation is so great as to have such righteous decrees and laws as this body of laws I am setting before you today? [9] Only be careful, and watch yourselves closely so that you do not forget the things your eyes have seen or let them slip from your heart as long as you live. **Teach them to your children and to their children after them**.*

We must no longer think that a public school, or college education is enough. It is not enough and the current curriculum being taught is not what God intended. We are on a collision course with the judgment of the Almighty.

We must begin to learn the principles of the four God ordained institutions and begin obeying their stipulations. (Self-Government / Family Government / Church Government / Civil Government)

Every individual has a responsibility to know and teach the institutions and their Biblical requirements. Every single person can voice their opinion and place their vote for God to return to our schools. We all originated from a family, we are part of a family and we can disciple our family as well as those around us in righteousness.

I would like to make a note that I will develop more in civil government. Eventually, public education needs to be removed from the control of the government and again placed in the hands of the family and church. It is ok to supplement your parental education with Christian education from a school or system, but it still does not replace the fact that each parent needs to be teaching their children the Word. We must return to that requirement and speak up for those in the public school system.

If we will invest in our children and teach them the institutions and teach them how to correctly handle the Word of God as they go out into the world they can disciple the nation. This is God's intent to having a godly nation. We all must do our part. We must raise a generation of the upright. Currently in our home we have five children and each child, most likely, represents a family. As we raise these children we are not only affecting their lives but we are affecting our children's children and the generation that they will live in.

What will America look like in 50 years if we do not return to God and His Word? At what point will God destroy us as He has done to all the nations before us who would not obey His commands?

Psalm 112:1-2 (NIV) [1] **Praise the LORD. Blessed is the man who fears the LORD, who finds great delight in his commands.** [2] **His children will be mighty in the land; the generation of the upright will be blessed.**

Will you delight yourself in the Word and impress the Word to your children?

Will your children be mighty in the land?

Even if your children are no longer in the home you can begin teaching them the principles and encouraging them to pass on the faith. Even if you are single and do not currently have children you are responsible for you still have a voice when it comes to electing officials. You also have influence with your own family members and those around you to encourage them to return to the ways of God.

WORKSHEET FOR FAMILY GOVERNMENT
LIFE TRUTH # I
THE FAMILY IS GOD'S DESIGN

Question: What is God's design for a family?
Answer: God's design for a family is one man, one woman and their children.

> *Mark 10:6-8 (NIV)* [6] *"But at the beginning of creation God 'made them male and female.'* [7] *'For this reason a man will leave his father and mother and be united to his wife,* [8] *and the two will become one flesh.' So they are no longer two, but one.*

> Write out the Life Truth, question, and answer on one side of an index card and the verse on the other side. Keep it in your Bible for the week. Work on it every day individually and as a family. Have it memorized by next week.

According to Mark 10:6-8. What is God's design for a family?
One M_____ and One W_____

Read Deuteronomy 11:13-17. What do we need to be doing in order to experience the blessings of God's provisions? (rain, grass, food, etc...)

Read Deuteronomy 11:18-21. What words are we to fix in our hearts and minds?

Do you think Scripture memory is a part of fixing the Word in our hearts?　　　　If yes, how often are you memorizing Scripture with your children?

Who is responsible to teach the children?

Read Deuteronomy 11:22-28. God promises to protect us from enemies when we are doing what?

Read Matthew 19:13-15. How does Jesus view children?

The Bible tells us in *Matthew 22:37-38 (NIV)* *[37] Jesus replied: "'Love the Lord your God with all your heart and with all your soul and with all your mind.' [38] This is the first and greatest commandment.*

Family Government: Be in the Word and prayer with my family everyday / Memorize Scripture with my children / Train them to walk in righteousness
On a scale of 1 to 10 how is your family doing in these areas?
Poor   Great
1 2   3   4   5   6   7   8   9   10

Based on this LIFE TRUTH what commitments do you need to make in the area family government? What commitments will you make this week as a family?

FAMILY-GOVERNMENT
LIFE TRUTH # 2
A FATHER'S RESPONSIBILITIES

Bees are amazing creatures that were created by God to make honey. In a bee community, there are specific roles that bees must fulfill in order for them to reproduce and make honey. The honey that they make is necessary to sustain them during the winter. God designed bees to go from plant to plant to collect pollen and oils to make the honey as well as to fertilize many other plants in the process. What would happen to plants if bees did not fulfill their designated roles? Plants would not reproduce and eventually would die out.

As in the bee community, God has created each individual to fulfill a specific purpose in this life. It is through his Word, that man can know and understand how to fulfill this purpose. Although God's plans are always best, we have been given a choice whether or not to obey them. If we choose to obey His commands, we will begin to see His blessings pour out upon our nation.

Fathers have a huge responsibility when it comes to the health of a nation; as the family goes so goes the nation. The health of a church and the health of a nation are dependent upon the health of families. Fathers need to fulfill their God-given roles and lead their families in the way God intended for them to do. By doing this, they will help lead this nation into righteousness.

Our nation has taken its eyes off of the Word of God. We have placed our wants and desires ahead of our God-given family responsibilities. We must return to God in order for our nation to be healed. A nation is made up of families. The leaders of nations are trained first in their families. Look at what God said about Abraham in *Genesis 18:18-19 (NIV)* *[18] Abraham will surely become a great and powerful nation, and all nations on earth will be blessed through him. [19] For **I have chosen him, so that he will direct his children and his household after him to keep the way of the LORD** by doing what is right and just, so that the LORD will bring about for Abraham what he has promised him."*

The Bible says that from Abraham's family comes *"**a great and powerful nation, and all nations on earth will be blessed through him.**"* God's design is for families to come together and form a powerful nation that is then able to bless others. Verse nineteen reveals to us how this plan is to be a reality. The father is to *"direct his children and his household to keep the way of the Lord."* He is not only responsible for his household to keep the way of the Lord, but the households after him are to keep the way of the Lord. If we will keep the way of the Lord and train our households to do the same, then the Lord will bring about what he has promised.

We need men to submit themselves to the Lordship of Jesus; godly men, who will commit and return to the ways of God according to His Word. We need fathers who know and understand their God-given responsibilities and who will fulfill them in order for our nation to be blessed again.

We need men like Joshua who led his home and encouraged other families to do the same. *Joshua 24:14-15 (NIV)* [14] *"**Now fear the LORD and serve him with all faithfulness**. Throw away the gods your forefathers worshiped beyond the River and in Egypt, and serve the LORD.* [15] *But if serving the LORD seems undesirable to you, then choose for yourselves this day whom you will serve, whether the gods your forefathers served beyond the River, or the gods of the Amorites, in whose land you are living. But as for me and my household, we will serve the LORD."*

What will your household do? Will you fear the Lord and serve Him?

Our households must get in order before our nation will be in order. These are some statistics from fatherless homes:

- 63% of youth suicides are from fatherless homes (US Dept. Of Health/Census)
- 90% of all homeless and runaway children are from fatherless homes

- 85% of all children who show behavior disorders come from fatherless homes (Center for Disease Control)
- 80% of rapists come from fatherless homes (Justice & Behavior, Vol. 14, p. 403-26)
- 71% of all high school dropouts come from fatherless homes (National Principals Association Report)
- 85% of all youths sitting in prisons grew up in a fatherless home. (Source: Fulton County Georgia jail populations, Texas Dept. Of Corrections, 1992).

The Bible says that men are to be the heads of their homes. Unfortunately, many times men want to rule their homes like the Gentiles did when they would lord over their people. But as we learned in Self-Government, we are to be servant leaders. This is especially true in the home. Do you remember the "*I am created to serve*" verse? It says in Mark 10:43-44 (NIV) [43] *Not so with you. Instead, whoever wants to become great among you must be your servant,* [44] *and whoever wants to be first must be slave of all.*"

Here are seven important responsibilities of a godly father:

1. FATHERS FEAR THE LORD

Joshua 24:14-15 (NIV) [14] **"Now fear the LORD and serve him with all faithfulness**. This is an area of self-government and it must be the first thing all of us do. We must learn to govern ourselves under the Lordship of Jesus and His Holy Word.

Look at what Jeremiah says in *Jeremiah 32:38-40 (NIV)* [38] *They will be my people, and I will be their God.* [39] *I will give them singleness of heart and action,* **so that they will <u>always</u> fear me for their own good and the good of their children after them.** [40] *I will make an everlasting covenant with them:* <u>**I will never stop doing good to them**</u>, *and I will* **inspire them to fear me, so that they will never turn away from me.**

Blessings from God upon America have diminished greatly. We are seeing the curses all around us. The Word says if we obey God, He will never stop doing good to us. The key to God blessing us is our obedience to His Word.

Part of our corrupt nature is that we do not fear God. Romans, Chapter 3, gives us a description of what we are like without God. In *Romans 3:18 (NIV)* [18] *"There is no fear of God before their eyes."* Salvation gives us a new nature and the ability to fear the Lord. We must walk in the fear of God and turn away from the corrupt flesh.

What if someone hired you to tend their garden? They told you to prepare the soil, plant the seeds, tend the garden, and pick the produce. If they hired you and said they had to go out of town and wouldn't be back until right after the harvest, would you be a faithful worker and fulfill the task that you have been hired to do? When the owner returns, would you have produce to show for your hard work so the owner would be pleased with you?

This analogy can be addressed to us spiritually. When God returns what will He find that we have done? Will He find the "produce" that He requires? Will the fruit of obeying God be evident in our families and in our nation? Will He find us working on His garden or will He find that we have been busy doing our own things?

Jesus is going to return. He is going to judge us according to what we have done based upon His will for our lives. Fathers, it is vital that we lead in the fear of the Lord. It is vital that we show our families that we are concerned about God finding us faithful when He returns.

Psalm 111:10 (NIV) [10] **The fear of the LORD is the beginning of wisdom**; *all who follow his precepts have good understanding. To him belongs eternal praise.*

The husband is the head of the home. It is his responsibility to lead his family to fear the Lord. As the passage in Jeremiah says, *"it is for our own good that we fear the Lord."* As the family goes so goes the nation. As the father goes so goes the family.

Fathers need to walk in a state of knowing that everything they do will be judged by God. Their words, their actions, and even their thoughts will be revealed at the judgment. It is important for fathers to walk in righteousness and teach their children to do the same. If it were possible to know how soon we would be standing before God and answering for our lives, I think we would be spending a lot more time confessing our sins and making sure that we did not sin until our appointed time. The Bible says that we should always be ready. It says in *Hebrews 9:27 (NIV) [27] Just as man is destined to die once, and after that to face judgment* . We all have an appointed time to stand before God.

2. FATHERS SEEK THE KNOWLEDGE OF GOD

When Solomon was made King of Israel, it became his responsibility to lead the nation of Israel. He cried out to God for wisdom and knowledge to lead the people. *2 Chronicles 1:8-12 (NIV) [8] Solomon answered God, "You have shown great kindness to David my father and have made me king in his place. [9] Now, LORD God, let your promise to my father David be confirmed, for you have made me king over a people who are as numerous as the dust of the earth. [10]* **Give me wisdom and knowledge, that I may lead this people, for who is able to govern this great people of yours?"** *[11] God* said to Solomon, "Since this is your heart's desire and you have not asked for wealth, riches or honor, nor for the death of your enemies, and since you have not asked for a long life but for wisdom and knowledge to govern my people over whom I have made you king, *12 therefore wisdom and knowledge will be given you. And I will also give you wealth, riches and honor, such as no king who was before you ever had and none after you will have."* If you are a father, then God is expecting you to lead and govern your family. God does not create mistakes. If He has blessed you with children, then He knows you can raise them. But He also knows that you need Him to accomplish the task. We should be crying out to God for wisdom and knowledge to lead our families. God does not want to hide His wisdom from us. He promises to give it to those who ask Him. *James 1:5-8 (NIV) 5 **If any of you lacks wisdom, he should ask God, who gives generously to all without finding fault, and it will be given to him.** 6 But when he asks, he must believe and not doubt, because he who doubts is like a wave of the sea, blown and tossed by the wind. 7 That man should not think he will receive anything from the Lord; 8 he is a double-minded man, unstable in all he does.*

We should be asking God for wisdom and knowledge every day. He also expects us to search for His wisdom. *Proverbs 2:1-10 (NIV) 1 **My son, if you accept my words and store up my commands within you,** 2 turning your ear to wisdom and applying your heart to understanding, 3 and if you call out for insight and cry aloud for understanding, 4 and if you look* *for it as for silver and search for it as for hidden treasure,* *⁵ then you will understand the fear of the LORD and find the knowledge of God.* *⁶ For the LORD gives wisdom, and from his mouth come knowledge and understanding.* *⁷ He holds victory in store for the upright, he is a shield to those whose walk is blameless,* *⁸ for he guards the course of the just and protects the way of his faithful ones.* *⁹ Then you will understand what is right and just and fair–every good path.* *¹⁰ For wisdom will enter your heart, and knowledge will be pleasant to your soul.* We must be continually searching the Scriptures for wisdom and understanding. Fathers, we must be storing God's Word in our hearts. **That means memorizing, meditating, and applying God's truths to our lives.**

If you are not interested in the Word, then it is very probable that your family will not be interested in the Word. Families should see their fathers reading the Word. Families should hear their fathers quoting the Scriptures. Families should hear their fathers reading the Scriptures. Families should hear their fathers sharing practical ways to apply the Word of God to their lives. Too many men start reading the Word and then quit way too early. Don't give up! Get into a Bible study. Pray before you read God's Word and ask for wisdom.
Fathers, the family sees what we love. We talk about what we love. We invest our time, energy, and money into what we love. Our relationship with God should be our highest investment. Everything we do should relate to our fear of the Lord.

3. FATHERS ARE TO BE THE MAIN PROVIDERS

In Self Government Life Truth number 10: *"I am created to work"*, we learned that we are created to work and to be productive members of society. God expects us to work and earn the bread that we eat. We are not to be dependent upon anyone. Men are not to be taking money for their livelihood from the government or anyone else. Men are to be the main providers for their homes. Men are commanded by God to provide for their families. *I Timothy 5:8 (NIV) [8] If anyone does not provide for his relatives, and especially for his immediate family, he has denied the faith and is worse than an unbeliever.*

Fathers are to work hard and store up provisions for their families. This is not so their families can be lazy. It is so their families can be prepared for emergencies and unexpected troubles that often happen in this world.

Proverbs 13:22 (NIV) [22] A good man leaves an inheritance for his children's children, but a sinner's wealth is stored up for the righteous.

2 Corinthians 12:14b (NIV) After all, children should not have to save up for their parents, but parents for their children.

Yes, you will have to work through the pain and soreness that these corrupted bodies go through.

Yes, there will be days when you do not want to get up and days when you would rather go fishing. But the reality is that God has called you to be the main provider for the home. Remember what God said to Adam after the fall? *Genesis 3:17-19 (NIV) ¹⁷ To Adam he said, "Because you listened to your wife and ate from the tree about which I commanded you, 'You must not eat of it,' "Cursed is the ground because of you; through* **painful toil** *you will eat of it all the days of your life. ¹⁸ It will produce thorns and thistles for you, and you will eat the plants of the field. ¹⁹* **By the sweat of your brow** *you will eat your food until you return to the ground, since from it you were taken; for dust you are and to dust you will return."*

After the fall, work became harder. Our bodies get tired, but that is not an excuse for us to be idle or to be dependent upon anyone. We are to be productive in society and we are to work for the bread we eat.

4. FATHERS ARE THE PROTECTORS

One of the main responsibilities of a father is to protect his family from Satan and the tricks Satan uses to deceive them. A father has a great responsibility to present his wife and children before the Lord holy and blameless. *Ephesians 5:22-27 (NIV) ²² Wives, submit to your husbands as to the Lord. ²³ For the husband is the head of the wife as Christ is the head of the church, his body, of which he is the Savior. ²⁴ Now as the church submits to Christ, so also wives should submit to their husbands in everything. ²⁵ Husbands, love*

42

your wives, just as Christ loved the church and gave himself up for her *26* to make her holy, cleansing her by the washing with water through the word, *27* and to present her to himself as a radiant church, without stain or wrinkle or any other blemish, but holy and blameless.*

Listen to how the Lord described Job as a father. *Job 1:8 (NIV) 8 Then the LORD said to Satan, "Have you considered my servant Job? There is no one on earth like him; he is blameless and upright, **a man who fears God and shuns evil**."* Are your children shunning evil? Are you protecting your home from evil influences that seek to draw them away from their devotion to the Lord? Do your children have a healthy fear of the Lord? Is it enough that they will shun evil?

Job covered his family with prayer, which is one of our greatest weapons. *Job 1:4-5 (NIV) 4 His sons used to take turns holding feasts in their homes, and they would invite their three sisters to eat and drink with them. 5 When a period of feasting had run its course, Job would send and have them purified. Early in the morning he would sacrifice a burnt offering for each of them, thinking, "Perhaps my children have sinned and cursed God in their hearts." This was Job's regular custom.*

Fathers must pray for their children and seek to protect their hearts. Fathers must engage their children in tough conversations about holiness based upon God's Word. Fathers must watch out for warning signs of selfishness, pride, and a hardened hearts towards God and His Word. Fathers must be prayerfully concerned if their children have no desire to read God's Word. (Psalm 1)

A father needs to lead out in the Self Government truths and apply them to his own life. Encouragement helps children not to have hardened hearts.

Remember the verse from *Hebrews 3:13 (NIV)* [13] *But encourage one another daily, as long as it is called Today, so that none of you may be hardened by sin's deceitfulness.* If fathers love the Word of God, and encourage their families to do the same, our nation will see a return to God.

When fathers are the heroes of the home, their children will look up to them for guidance and instruction.

5. FATHERS ARE A GODLY EXAMPLE

The Lord said of Job that he was a man, "*who fears God and shuns evil.*" Would the Lord say the same of us? Would our children say the same of us? We must lead by example. If we are not fulfilling the responsibility of obeying God-given authority, then how can we expect our children to do the same? It is evil to say one thing and then do another. Our yes must be yes and our no must be no.

The greatest influence in a child's life is their parents. Other people can teach and train them, but children will more than likely follow their parents lead. That is why church ministries must be supplemental to the family's roles. You can bus kids into Sunday School and youth programs, but children, over 90% of the time, will follow their parents' examples. Dads and moms have the greatest influence on their children which is exactly how God designed it. We have all seen it in the eyes of young children when they look into their parent's eyes and long to be just like dad and mom.

The Lord requires fathers to raise their families to be holy and blameless in God's sight. Fathers are going to stand before God someday and answer for this God-given responsibility.

6. FATHERS LOVE THEIR WIVES

When males are thinking only about themselves and their own pleasures, they are generally not faithful to the marriage bed. They are not concerned about standing before God one day and giving an account for their lives. Notice I called them males and not men. Upright and godly men obey the Word of God. They heed God's commandments. Males who disobey God, not only bring judgment upon themselves, but also upon the nation and the generations after them.

Deuteronomy 5:7-10 (NIV) *[7] "You shall have no other gods before me. [8] "You shall not make for yourself an idol in the form of anything in heaven above or on the earth beneath or in the waters below. [9] You shall not bow down to them or worship them; for I, the LORD your God, am a jealous God,* **punishing the children for the sin of the fathers to the third and fourth generation of those who hate me,** [10] <u>but showing love to a thousand [generations] of those who love me and keep my commandments.</u>

Men are to remain pure until their wedding day and they are to remain faithful to the wife of their youth.

Men fear God and do all they can to please Him.

Men remain faithful to their wives and children and they stick it out through the hard times because God hates divorce. (Malachi 2:16)

In the first part of the wives and husbands passage in Ephesians 5, it says *Ephesians 5:25-26 (NIV)* [25] *Husbands, love your wives, just as Christ loved the church and gave himself up for her* [26] *to make her holy, cleansing her by the washing with water through the word,*

Fathers are to be the example in holiness. Husbands are called to love their wives sacrificially, as Christ loved the church. The passage goes on to explain this sacrificial love for our wives.

Ephesians 5:28-33 (NIV) [28] *In this same way, husbands ought to love their wives as their own bodies. He who loves his wife loves himself.* [29] *After all, no one ever hated his own body, but he feeds and cares for it, just as Christ does the church–* [30] *for we are members of his body.* [31]

"For this reason a man will leave his father and mother and be united to his wife, and the two will become one flesh." [32] *This is a profound mystery—but I am talking about Christ and the church.* [33] *However, each one of you also must love his wife as he loves himself, and the wife must respect her husband.*

We are told to love our wives as much as we love ourselves. We are told to be concerned about the needs of our wives and are commanded to meet those needs. Men, stop being overly concerned about your own needs and start ministering to the needs of your wives; study her; pursue her; listen to her. From our Self-Government study we learned that we are created to serve, praise, encourage, witness, forgive, be holy, and work. If we are obeying our self-government responsibilities, we will be serving, praising, encouraging, and forgiving our wives.

Fathers, if we were concerned for our wives as much as we are about feeding ourselves, our wives would be satisfied and lack nothing. Most men do not miss a meal. When they are hungry, they do something about it. The Word tells us to be as concerned for our wives as we are about our own needs.

7. FATHER'S TRAIN THEIR CHILDREN

We should not be surprised at the many scandals that are happening in the leadership of our nation. As long as we have a godless educational system, and as long as we have families not taking the responsibility for raising the righteous, we will continue to see moral failures in the leadership of our nation.

When John the Baptist came on the scene, the nation of Israel was in a mess. The Roman Government was very oppressive and the church leaders were also corrupt. Jesus spoke to both of them and left us many teachings about how to govern our lives. John's message was to prepare the way for the Lord. He said in *Luke 1:17 (NIV) [17] And he will go on before the Lord, in the spirit and power of Elijah,* **to turn the hearts of the fathers to their children and the disobedient to the wisdom of the righteous--***to make ready a people prepared for the Lord."* Revival turns the hearts of fathers toward their children. Many males have kids but only men raise their children. Godly fathers raise their children with their primary concern being the salvation of their families.

Fathers discipline in love. *Proverbs 13:24 (NIV) [24] He who spares the rod hates his son, but he who loves him is careful to discipline him. Proverbs 19:18 (NIV) [18] Discipline your son, for in that there is hope; do not be a willing party to his death.* A father disciplines their children as God disciplines us, not in harshness or in frustration, but with love and concern for their souls. *Hebrews 12:7-8 (NIV) [7] Endure hardship as discipline; God is treating you as sons.* **For what son is not disciplined by his father?** *[8] If you are not disciplined (and everyone undergoes discipline), then you are illegitimate children and not true sons.*

When a father disciplines out of anger or frustration, it only harms and embitters a child. It provokes them to more anger and discouragement. When a father disciplines, not as a fellow sinner, but as someone sinless, it comes across as hypocrisy. We need to discipline in love, because without Christ, we ourselves could not obey.

Ephesians 6:4 (NIV) ⁴ Fathers, do not exasperate your children; instead, bring them up in the training and instruction of the Lord.

To exasperate is to enrage or entice to anger. It is also to irritate and annoy. Father's must realize that children are born with a corrupt nature and they must be trained. Training is the responsibility of the parents and requires education as well as patience.

Our children should know that we love them and that we are concerned about their souls. Many parents think that love is materialism. Materialism is a sin. Love is not a sin. **Love is a concern for their character more than a concern for their happiness.** Happiness might come temporarily through things, but we are told to train up the righteous. **The righteous are concerned more about others than they are about their own happiness.**

Fathers should be using the Scriptures to train their children. The Bible says in *2 Timothy 3:16-17 (NIV)* ¹⁶

All Scripture *is God-breathed and is useful for teaching, rebuking, correcting and training in righteousness,* [17] *so that the man of God may be thoroughly equipped for every good work.* **If a Father is not using the Scriptures to train his children, then he is failing in his God-given role as the head of the home.**

Our generation needs:

- Fathers who will fear the Lord.
- Fathers who will be faithful and love only one woman.
- Fathers who will be productive in society and provide for their families.
- Fathers who will seek the Word of God for knowledge and educate their children accordingly.

WORKSHEET FOR FAMILY GOVERNMENT LIFE TRUTH # 2 – A FATHER'S RESPONSIBILITIES

Question: What is God's design for a father?
Answer: God's design for a father is to love his wife, and bring his children up in the training and instruction of the Lord.

Ephesians 6:4 (NIV) ⁴ Fathers, do not exasperate your children; instead, bring them up in the training and instruction of the Lord.

> Write out the Life Truth, question, and answer on one side of an index card and the verse on the other side. Keep it in your Bible for the week. Work on it every day individually and as a family. Have it memorized by next week.

To exasperate is to enrage or entice to anger. It is also to irritate and annoy. Father's must realize that children are born with a corrupt nature and they must be trained. According to Ephesians 6:4. What kinds of things should a father be doing to train and instruct his children?

How does 2 Timothy 3:16,17 relate to how a father should train his children?

Read Exodus 34:1-7. How long does God punish the sin of fathers who do not repent?

Read I Samuel 2:12-17 What does the Bible call Eli's sons? V12

Read I Samuel 2:22-29. How was Eli participating in the sin that his sons were committing? V29

Read I Samuel 2:30-36. What was the judgment on Eli's family line?
There will n_____ be an old man
His descendants will be b_____ in their eyes from tears.
All his descendants will d_____ in the prime of life.

The sin of Eli, as the father and the priest, was grievous to God. Who else suffered because of Eli's disobedience? (I Samuel 2:31-33)

Read I Samuel 4:12-22. Verse 18 tells us that Eli was heavy. Why was Eli heavy?

What should Eli have done differently according to these three passages?

Proverbs13:24
Ephesians 6:4
Proverbs 25:28

Based on this LIFE TRUTH what commitments do you need to make to help fathers be the men that God has called them to be? What commitments will you make this week as a family?

FAMILY-GOVERNMENT LIFE TRUTH # 3 A MOTHER'S RESPONSIBILITIES

There are many things that are attacking the family in our generation. We are seeing a breakdown in family values and in the responsibilities of parents according to their God ordained roles. Parents are not sure what their biblical roles are and society is many times telling us to do the opposite of what God expects of us. Satan has a goal to destroy marriages and families because when he does he can destroy a nation. Feminism is an organized movement to demand equal rights for women. It may have begun with good intentions enabling women to vote, work, and other such equalities, but in many ways it has moved beyond the Biblical role for women. It is good for a movement to defend the cause of helpless women and ban rape, human trafficking, and other immoralities. But, it is sin when we move away from the Bible and its commands.

God's Word is what should govern us. Unfortunately, there are times when we, as humans, cause inequality within races, sexes and nationalities. The Scriptures declare that we are all of the same race and those in Christ are all heirs to the promise. *Galatians 3:28-29 (NIV)* *[28] There is neither Jew nor Greek, slave nor free, male nor female, for you are all one in Christ Jesus. [29] If you belong to Christ, then you are Abraham's seed, and heirs according to the promise.* **This teaching of**

equality does not negate the biblical roles that God intends for us. A father has certain responsibilities and mothers have specific responsibilities.

God is the creator and the designer of everything. *Colossians 1:16 (NIV)* *[16] For by him (Jesus) all things were created: things in heaven and on earth, visible and invisible, whether thrones or powers or rulers or authorities; all things were created by him and for him.* God decided who would be male and who would be female. To go against God's design would be rebellion against Him.

Feminism now demands equal rights for women in ways that go against God's design for a healthy society. Tragically, the feminist movement seeks to belittle the Biblical role of wife / mother and puts great pressure on women to demand equal rights with men in all things. Satan is using this movement to call the Biblical wife outdated and old fashioned. We must be very careful to return to the God ordained institution of family and understand what God's Word says in our roles.

It is within our corrupt nature that we do not want to submit to authority, but all of us must submit to Christ. Blessings follow the family who will obey God and His principles. Blessings follow the nation as families submit to God and fulfill His intentions for them.

Being a mother has huge responsibilities and expectations that no man can fulfill. To pervert the role of motherhood is to cause confusion upon the generations behind us. Healthy nations fulfill their roles and continue on for the generations to come. One Biblical command for the family is to be fruitful and fill the earth. If a society decides to no longer obey this command eventually, the society would be no more.

Jesus has always been a supporter of women's rights and certain equalities for all. In the Old Testament Law it protected women from rape, made sure they would be supported if their husbands died or divorced them, and gave them a place to worship God. These rights were unheard of in societies of that time.

Jesus actions were radical as well. He ignored cultural pressures and did what no rabbi, priest, or Pharisee would have dared done in that generation. He forgave the woman caught in the act of adultery (John 8:1-11). He spoke to a Samaritan woman (John 4:4-42). He ministered to an unclean woman (Matthew 9:20-22).

Jesus has designed women to be a part of His awesome plan in society. Even before sin entered our world God established His plan for the woman. *Genesis 2:18 (NIV)* *[18] The LORD God said, "It is not good for the man to be alone. I will make **a helper suitable for him**."* God's intent from the beginning was for the woman to be a helper to the man. Some might say that just Eve was created to be the helper, but this is not just for Adam and Eve but this is the establishment of the Family institution. The passage in Genesis continues.

Genesis 2:20-24 (NIV) [20] *So the man gave names to all the livestock, the birds of the air and all the beasts of the field. But for Adam no suitable helper was found.* [21] *So the LORD God caused the man to fall into a deep sleep; and while he was sleeping, he took one of the man's ribs and closed up the place with flesh.* [22] *Then the LORD God made a woman from the rib he had taken out of the man, and he brought her to the man.* [23] *The man said, "This is now bone of my bones and flesh of my flesh; she shall be called 'woman,' for she was taken out of man."* [24] *For this reason a man will leave his father and mother and be united to his wife, and they will become one flesh.*

The plan for a society is for men and women to come together and form a family government. In the responsibilities for the husband we learned that He is the head of the wife. She is the helper to the man to form the government of their family. In every institution there are authorities. As individuals self-governing ourselves we have the authority to choose what we do. There are consequences and blessings for our choices but God has created us with the freedom to choose and rule our lives.

In the family the Dad is the head of the home and he is responsible for the health of his family. In the church Christ is the head of the church and He has decided to establish leaders to govern the church body. In Civil government God appoints people to lead and gives them authority to rule over a society. Who decided that the woman should be the helper? God did! If we don't like the fact that women are created as the helpers for man who are we going against? Satan has caused such a stir in our nation that some women, even in the church, don't like this role and rebel against it.

It is true that some men have distorted the Biblical role of head of the home to mean a tyrant and sought to place women in a slave like role. But just because certain men have distorted their role does not negate the role that God has called the wife and mothers too. Men are called to love their wives as Christ loves the church. Sacrificially, gently, patiently, and as a man sold out to one woman alone! His eyes should light up every time he sees her because of his great love for her!

Women are called to be under the headship of the men that they marry. This is why it is so important to raise our daughters in the understanding that one day they will be married to a man and be under his authority. We should be doing all that we can to teach them what qualities a godly man will have. What if a woman gets married to a man and he is not a believer. What should she do? Should she divorce him? The Bible says no. *I Corinthians 7:13 (NIV) [13] And if a woman has a husband who is not a believer and he is* willing to live with her, she must not divorce him. It goes on to say, *I Corinthians 7:15-16 (NIV)* *15 But if the unbeliever leaves, let him do so. A believing man or woman is not bound in such circumstances; God has called us to live in peace. 16 How do you know, wife, whether you will save your husband? Or, how do you know, husband, whether you will save your wife?*

We are not to marry hoping that our spouses will get saved we are to marry Christians and raise a righteous generation. What if the unbelieving husband does not want to leave? *I Peter 3:1-6 (NIV) 1 Wives, in the same way be submissive to your husbands so that, if any of them do not believe the word, they may be won over without words by the behavior of their wives, 2 when they see the purity and reverence of your lives. 3 Your beauty should not come from outward adornment, such as braided hair and the wearing of gold jewelry and fine clothes. 4 Instead, it should be that of your inner self, the unfading beauty of a gentle and quiet spirit, which is of great worth in God's sight. 5 **For this is the way the holy women of the past who put their hope in God used to make themselves beautiful. They were submissive to their own husbands**, 6 like Sarah, who obeyed Abraham and called him her master. You are her daughters if you do what is right and do not give way to fear.*

Wives are called to be gentle, quiet, and submissive to their husbands. Their Christ like servant behavior will win their husbands over. In such a marriage, it will not be the constant words and preaching of a wife that will win the husband over but the gentle, quiet, submissive wife. If women are called to submit to their unbelieving husbands, in this way, how much more then to the believing husband?

What causes women not to want to submit to their husbands and follow their lead? Our selfish nature, our corrupt nature that we learned in Self Government we must crucify. Look at these passages: *Ephesians 5:24 (NIV) [24] Now as the church submits to Christ, so also wives should submit to their husbands in everything. Colossians 3:18 (NIV) [18] Wives, submit to your husbands, as is fitting in the Lord.*
In our flesh, as we read such passages, it can be like scrapping our fingers slowly across a chalk board. It can cause us to rise up and say, "no way, I don't want to do that." We must remember that we can trust God and know that He has our best in mind.
To submit to your husband is to <u>empower him to be the servant leader</u> that God has called him to be. If you were putting a car engine together you would want to make sure that you had all the parts. As the parts went together you would notice that they all have a part to play in making the engine run. If you decided to leave one of the main parts off, the engine would not run. In the same way, God has designed how a family will run best. He knows how the family is made and what it will take to fulfill the families role in society.

I will make a note here. If you are a wife and your husband is treating you emotionally or physically abusive God has not called you to remain silent and to be abused. You need to tell your pastor or a trusted love someone that can help you or even get you out of danger, if necessary.

God will never ask you to do something that he would not do himself. God calls the wife to be a helper and the Scriptures declare that God Himself is our helper. To be a helper is to be Christ-like. Wives need to understand the potential that they have for good or for evil. A woman can use her influence with men to build up or to tear down. If you have an unbelieving husband apply the principles of 1 Peter chapter 3. If you have a husband who is not yet leading in Spiritual matters pray earnestly for him and tame the tongue from any negative words. Encourage him in what he is doing for you and the family and use your influence to help him fulfill his God given responsibilities. Submit to his authority and encourage him to lead.

Esther was a wife who used her influence to save the nation of Israel (Book of Esther), while Delilah was a woman who brought Samson down and had him thrown into prison (Judges 16). Each woman used her influence one for good and the other for evil. Wives God has created you to come alongside your husbands and use your influence to build him up. God desires that you minister together and work together as one. You have a choice. You can either use your influence in your home toward godliness or for evil.

Eve used her influence in the life of Adam to cause both of them to sin.

Wives need to learn the principles of Self-Government and begin applying them in her home. She does not need to be a faultfinder but she needs to be an encourager. She needs to move away from complaining and begin to praise the Lord. She needs to learn how to respect her husband. *Ephesians 5:33 (NIV) 33 However, each one of you also must love his wife as he loves himself, and the wife must respect her husband.*

Men need their wives to respect them. Thank them for what they are doing right and pray for them in the areas that need work. Look at this passage in *Proverbs 21:9 (NIV) 9 Better to live on a corner of the roof than share a house with a quarrelsome wife.* Just in case we missed that verse in chapter 21 God had it repeated in chapter 25. *Proverbs 25:24 (NIV) 24 Better to live on a corner of the roof than share a house with a quarrelsome wife.*

The Bible says this about Delilah just before she broke him down and he finally told her his secret. *Judges 16:16 (NIV) 16 With such nagging she prodded him day after day until he was tired to death.* Wives can do the opposite and encourage their husbands day after day in order for them to be the empowered Christ-like servant leader of the home. The Proverbs also teach us *Proverbs 14:1 (NIV) 1 The wise woman builds her house, but with her own hands the foolish one tears hers down.* Women have the ability to empower their husbands to lead. If they become faultfinders they can tear their own homes down.

What are the responsibilities of a mother?

1. Cooperate in the Biblical Partnership

*I Peter 3:7 (NIV) ⁷ Husbands, in the same way be considerate as you live with your wives, and treat them with respect as the weaker **partner** and **as heirs with you** of the gracious gift of life, so that nothing will hinder your prayers.*

The Bible calls this relationship a partnership. We come together to form one flesh and we are joint heirs together with Christ. Yes, it does say that the woman is the weaker partner; it does say that woman is to be the helper to the man; it does say that the woman is to submit to their husbands; so get on board and join the partnership. Can we trust Jesus? Can we trust God's Word?

When we hear phrases like, "I am not going to submit to any man." Or "I am not going to be a helper to any man." Where are those phrases coming from? From Christ or from Satan?

It is the same as someone saying, "I am not going to obey God." When we decide that we are not going to submit to God and His ways we bring reproach to His name. We malign the Word of God by our disobedience. To malign is to discredit and bring an evil influence into society. Christians are to set the example in our obedience to God and as God blesses His people the world will take notice.

The mother is not submitting to a man so that he can do whatever he wants. The partnership is joining together with a man to form a godly family to raise a righteous generation. This is why it is so important for young men and women to grow up knowing God's will for their lives. To grow up and just marry anyone is not our calling. We are to come together with an Believer to establish a Christ centered family. This is the Biblical partnership of marriage.

2. Love your husband and children

Titus 2:3-5 (NIV) [3] *Likewise, teach the older women to be reverent in the way they live, not to be slanderers or addicted to much wine, but to teach what is good.* [4] *Then they can train the younger women to love their husbands and children,* [5] *to be self-controlled and pure, to be busy at home, to be kind, and to be subject to their husbands, so that no one will malign the word of God.* Verse four tells us that the older women are to train the younger women to love their husbands There are three levels of intimacy, emotional, spiritual, and physical.

In emotional intimacy spouses should meet each other's emotional needs for companionship and fill that gap of loneliness. Remember that God said, "It is not good for the man to be alone." Be best friends;

get to know one another; talk to one another and have fun together.

Spiritually a couple needs to come together in the Word and in prayer. It has been said that, "A couple who prays together stays together." Parents need to come together and pray for their homes and their children. They need to be in the Word together daily. The Scriptures tell us to be praying about everything.

Physically, spouses need to be meeting the physical needs of each other. *I Corinthians 7:3-5 (NIV)* [3] *The husband should fulfill his marital duty to his wife, and likewise the wife to her husband.* [4] *The wife's body does not belong to her alone but also to her husband. In the same way, the husband's body does not belong to him alone but also to his wife.* [5] *Do not deprive each other except by mutual consent and for a time, so that you may devote yourselves to prayer. Then come together again so that Satan will not tempt you because of your lack of self-control.*

You will notice in the command not to deprive each other except by mutual consent is also the command to devote ourselves to prayer.

Most women do not need to be reminded to love their children. It is a natural instinct that God has given them. Moms have a special comfort that only they can give to their children. *Isaiah 66:13 (NIV)* [13] *As a mother comforts her child, so will I comfort you; and you will be comforted over Jerusalem."*

3. Raise the righteous

As we talked about in the father's responsibilities we are to bring our children up in the training and instruction of the Lord. We learned that the family is also responsible for the education of their children. Men have a primary responsibility to be the main providers of the home which means the wife will be home more with the children. The Mother has a responsibility to teach the children as well. *Proverbs 1:8 (NIV) [8] Listen, my son, to your father's instruction and do not forsake your mother's teaching.*

Proverbs 6:20-22 (NIV) [20] My son, keep your father's commands and do not forsake your mother's teaching. [21] Bind them upon your heart forever; fasten them around your neck. [22] When you walk, they will guide you; when you sleep, they will watch over you; when you awake, they will speak to you.

Our greatest responsibility is not to acquire many material things and get a worldly education. Our main goal as a family is to raise the righteous who can in turn fulfill the gospel. The gospel is *Matthew 28:19-20 (NIV) [19] Therefore go and make disciples **of all nations,** baptizing them in the name of the Father and of the Son and of the Holy Spirit, [20] and **teaching them to obey everything I have commanded you.** And surely I am with you always, to the very end of the age."*

We get so excited and proud when our kids get good grades in their public education or at the colleges they attend. Getting good grades in a godless institution is not fulfilling the responsibility that God has given to parents. Yes, we should work hard at everything we do. Yes, if they are in public school they should be encouraged to make good grades and do their best, as if they were working unto the Lord. Yes, we should acknowledge their hard work and accomplishment. But parents this is not the main education God told us to give our children. As parents we are to teach our children the commands of God and all the teachings of Christ.

Matthew 5:17-20 (NIV) [17] *"Do not think that I have come to abolish the Law or the Prophets; I have not come to abolish them but to fulfill them.* [18] *I tell you the truth, until heaven and earth disappear, not the smallest letter, not the least stroke of a pen, will by any means disappear from the Law until everything is accomplished.* [19] *Anyone who breaks one of the least of these commandments and teaches others to do the same will be called least in the kingdom of heaven,* **but whoever practices and teaches these commands will be called great in the kingdom of heaven.** [20] *For I tell you that unless your righteousness surpasses that of the Pharisees and the teachers of the law, you will certainly not enter the kingdom of heaven.*

This is how a nation will be free and prosperous. Our children are to grow up and lead in the righteousness of our nation. They are to be an example and teach others the commands of Christ. We are to be exampling what a godly mother should be doing and then teaching our daughters to grow up and be godly mothers as well. *Titus 2:3-5 (NIV)* *³ Likewise, teach the older women to be reverent in the way they live, not to be slanderers or addicted to much wine,* **but to teach** *what is good.* *⁴ Then they can* **train the younger women** *to love their husbands and children,* *⁵ to be self-controlled and pure, to be busy at home, to be kind, and to be subject to their husbands, so that no one will malign the word of God.*

We need more Christian education going on in the lives of the children in our society. If our children were learning the Biblical principles then when they became leaders we would not be having all of the scandals that we are seeing today.

4. Manage the home

Does the Bible leave any room for a mother to work outside of the home? Yes it does. In what many call the Proverbs 31 woman there are several references to the wife working and earning her own profit for the household.

Proverbs 31:10-31 (NIV) *¹⁰ A wife of noble character who can find? She is worth far more than rubies.* *¹¹ Her husband has full confidence in her and lacks nothing of value.* *¹² She brings him good, not harm, all the days of her life.* *¹³ She selects wool and flax and works with eager* hands. ¹⁴ She is like the merchant ships, bringing her food from afar. ¹⁵ She gets up while it is still dark; she provides food for her family and portions for her servant girls. ¹⁶ **She considers a field and buys it; <u>out of her earnings</u> she plants a vineyard.** ¹⁷ She sets about her work vigorously; her arms are strong for her tasks. ¹⁸ She sees that **<u>her trading is profitable</u>**, and her lamp does not go out at night. ¹⁹ In her hand she holds the distaff and grasps the spindle with her fingers. ²⁰ She opens her arms to the poor and extends her hands to the needy. ²¹ When it snows, she has no fear for her household; for all of them are clothed in scarlet. ²² She makes coverings for her bed; she is clothed in fine linen and purple. ²³ Her husband is respected at the city gate, where he takes his seat among the elders of the land. ²⁴ **<u>She makes linen garments and sells them, and supplies the merchants with sashes</u>**. ²⁵ She is clothed with strength and dignity; she can laugh at the days to come. ²⁶ She speaks with wisdom, and faithful instruction is on her tongue. ²⁷ She watches over the affairs of her household and does not eat the bread of idleness. ²⁸ Her children arise and call her blessed; her husband also, and he praises her: ²⁹ "Many women do noble things, but you surpass them all." ³⁰ Charm is deceptive, and beauty is fleeting; but a woman who fears the LORD is to be praised. ³¹ Give her the reward she has earned, and let her works bring her praise at the city gate.

It is Biblical for a woman to supplement the income for the home but this is not the primary responsibility of the mother. One of a

mother's primary responsibilities is to be the manager of her home.

In the Proverbs 31 passage we also get a keen insight into the goal of raising the righteous. It says in verse *23 Her husband is respected at the city gate, where he takes his seat among the elders of the land.* The husband of this noble woman is in leadership in his community. The "city gate" would be symbolic of our current city halls. He is taking his seat of authority and responsibility with the other "elders" of the town. This is the goal of raising the righteous. No, not all of our righteous children will be in office, but our goal is that they would know what righteousness is and be able to vote correctly and then when they see injustice they would have the courage to speak up. We do need the righteous in office and we do need to be asking our children to ask God where he wants them to serve. If the righteous were governing the nation what would a society look like?

Some godly mother raised her son to be able to be at the "city gate." Not only was he ruling at the "city gate", but he chose a woman of noble character and now together they will raise another righteous generation. This is God's plan for families.
One of the character traits that the older women are to teach the younger is that of self-control. Do we really need the bigger house, the newer car, or to have the big vacations. Should we really be working so hard to buy more stuff or should we show restraint and be busy at home instilling in our

children the commands of God. *Joel 1:3 (NIV) ³ Tell it to your children, and let your children tell it to their children, and their children to the next generation.*
A godly wife is to be the manager of her home. This does not mean that she has to do all of the work but she is to manage and make sure her home is in order. From the Proverbs 31 woman it says, *¹⁵ She gets up while it is still dark; she provides food for her family and portions for her servant girls. And ²⁷ She watches over the affairs of her household and does not eat the bread of idleness.*

*Titus 2:3-5 (NIV) ³ Likewise, teach the older women to be reverent in the way they live, not to be slanderers or addicted to much wine, but to teach what is good. ⁴ Then they can train the younger women to love their husbands and children, ⁵ to be self-controlled and pure, **to be busy at home**, to be kind, and to be subject to their husbands, so that no one will malign the word of God.*

We learned that the husband has the ultimate responsibility to manage the home but his partner, who is to be busy at home, is to be his helpmate in this responsibility. The husband needs to know what is going on at home and help in the decisions of the home. He needs to be a part of the education process of His children. The wife should be sharing with the husband the issues that arise as she manages her household and seeks to raise the righteous. Look at this passage, *1 Timothy 5:14 (NIV) ¹⁴ So I counsel younger widows to marry, to have children, to **manage***

70

their homes *and to give the enemy no opportunity for slander.*

We are not to be raising "good" people we are to be raising the righteous. Part of managing the home is to make sure her children are growing up knowing the commands of God. Look at what it said again about the Proverbs 31 woman, [26] *She speaks with wisdom, and faithful instruction is on her tongue.*

We live in a society where many women have left the home to work full time jobs. Some women may have had to because of a divorce or because they have been widowed. But some women have chosen to leave the home so that they can purchase more. They have done this to the demise of our society.

Parents are responsible not to buy their children many materialistic things but to raise the righteous; Children who can quote God's Word; Children who can teach others how to obey the teachings of Christ; Children who have been trained to be leaders in society; Children who can sit at the "city gate" and rule righteously.

If we go to work and then we come home and we are too tired to invest in the Spiritual development of our children we are not fulfilling or designed roles. If we go to work and then come home and we run our children all around town to be involved in many activities this is not the designed role that God has given to us. We must slow down and fulfill what God is asking of us. Our nation is at stake. Our future is at stake. If we need to downsize and buy less to allow the mother to be able to stay home more and help educate the children then this is what needs to be done. God will not say, "Oh I noticed you had a big mortgage, a few car payments, and several activities you signed your children up for, so I exempted you from your responsibility to raise the righteous." John Jay who was one of the founders of our nation said, "Providence has given to our people the choice of their rulers, and it is the duty, as well as the privilege and interest, of our Christian nation to select and prefer Christians for their rulers." How will we elect Christians as our rulers when our society is not trying to raise righteous leaders? We currently have a godless educational system. We are to raise Christians who know the Word of God and they can quote it. Christians who live, act, and speak like Jesus.

We have a selfish society bent on greed, selfishness and the family is responsible. We must return to the roles that God has designed for us and obey God. Some women may say, "I cannot teach my children, I don't have a degree." "I'm not qualified." If God has given you children then He is expecting you to lean upon Him so that He can enable you to raise the righteous. God does not make mistakes. We must spend more time fulfilling our roles and stop chasing after our lusts. The church is following the patterns of the world and believing the lies of the feminist movement, but look at how this is destroying our nation.

Families must begin to spend more time teaching their children the Word of God. We must take our roles seriously as we seek to honor God with our lives. One reason women do not want to submit to their husbands is because we do not understand the biblical role of the family. The father is not the head of the home so that he can decide to do whatever he wants. The father is the head because he is to make sure that his family is raising the righteous and preparing them to make disciples "of all nations". That is a lot of work and he needs a partner who can help him fulfill that responsibility. Training is something that does not happen overnight. It takes a family daily meditating on the Word to raise the righteous.

This old fashion plan works and it will keep a nation free and under the blessings of God.
We need a reformation back to the will of God and mothers who will hear the voice of God and surrender to His authority. Women who will love their families, submit to their husbands, become the manger of their homes, and train up the righteous. Notice this verse from the Proverbs 31 woman.
Proverbs 31:30 (NIV) [30] Charm is deceptive, and beauty is fleeting; but a woman who fears the LORD is to be praised.

We need to fear the Lord and realize that we are not fulfilling our God given responsibilities. Our nation is suffering because of the lack of the Biblical knowledge of our children. Our nation is suffering because we are not raising our children to be the leaders of society. We are raising our children to go after things; diplomas, jobs, houses, cars, etc… But where are the righteous? Where are the preachers, senators, congressman, mayors, alderman, and missionaries?

Don't think that another family will raise the righteous to lead the land we all have that responsibility to raise the righteous.

WORKSHEET FOR FAMILY GOVERNMENT
LIFE TRUTH # 3
A MOTHER'S RESPONSIBILITIES

Question: What is God's design for a mother?
Answer: God's design for a mother is to empower her husband to lead, manage the home, and help raise the righteous.

Titus 2:3-5 (NIV) [3] Likewise, teach the older women to be reverent in the way they live, not to be slanderers or addicted to much wine, but to teach what is good. [4] Then they can train the younger women to love their husbands and children, [5] to be self-controlled and pure, to be busy at home, to be kind, and to be subject to their husbands, so that no one will malign the word of God.

> Write out the Life Truth, question, and answer on one side of an index card and the verse on the other side. Keep it in your Bible for the week. Work on it every day individually and as a family. Have it memorized by next week.

Read Genesis 2:15-24. God said that it was not good for the man to be alone so he created a
H_____ for the man.

Women have the power of influence in the lives of men. Read these passages and list if these women used their influence for good or for evil.
Read Genesis 3:1-6
Read Judges 16:4-21

Read Esther 4:12-14; 5:1-3; 7:1-10

Read Colossians 3:18. What are wives to do? Submission is empowering someone to lead. Wives are to use their influence to help their husbands lead in the home. In what ways could a wife empower her husband to lead?

In what ways could a wife tear down her husband in his being the head of a home?

Read 1 Timothy 5:14. Mothers are to be the M_____ of their homes. This week's memory verse also tells us that mothers are to be busy at home.

Circle the phrases that would be what God would want mothers to be doing at home.

- Running around constantly to various activities
- Training her children to be Christ-like
- Making sure the family is eating together
- Making sure her house is orderly
- Making sure her kids have all the toys they want
- Teaching her children the Word of God
- Raising her children to lead in society
- Complaining about laundry, dishes, etc…
- Having a daily quiet time
- Praying together as a family

Based on this LIFE TRUTH what commitments do you need to make to help mothers be the women that God has called them to be? What commitments will you make this week as a family?

FAMILY-GOVERNMENT
LIFE TRUTH # 4
CHILDREN'S RESPONSIBILITIES

What would a peaceful and content society look like? Could you describe it in a paragraph? What would people be doing or not doing? What would you notice about the character traits of people in such a society?

The nightly news depicts a society that is lacking in peace and contentment. God's Word has a plan for peace and contentment when a society submits to His commands. The Bible says in *Deuteronomy 5:29 (NIV)* [29] *Oh, that their hearts would be inclined to fear me and keep all my commands always,* ***so that it might go well with them and their children forever****!*

God's Word promises that if we submit to His commands it will go well with us forever! This shouldn't surprise us as we see the principles of order in His creation all around us. The sun fulfills its role. The rain and seasons have their purpose. Our God is a God of order and peace.

Perhaps it would help to understand each person's role by using an illustration from sports. What would happen in a football game if everyone decided to be the quarterback? There would be no one to snap the ball to the quarterback. There would be no blockers to defend the quarterback. There would be no one to hand or throw the ball to. A football team where everyone was the quarterback would not be successful. This illustration works with any team sport. We can clearly see the consequences of individuals not fulfilling their assigned roles on a team. But can we see the consequences in a society that doesn't fulfill their assigned roles?

What if you decided to build a house and all the contractors chose to only do the plumbing? Who would pour the foundation? Who would frame the walls and lay the roof? No one would buy a house with only plumbing, no matter how nice the plumbing was, and it would be embarrassing to use a bathroom with no walls!

Christians are to witness to every nation by following God's playbook. God's Word is our playbook! When we fulfill our assigned roles, God's Word promises that we will experience peace and contentment. *Deuteronomy 4:5-6 (NIV) [5] See, I have taught you decrees and laws as the LORD my God commanded me, so that you may follow them in the land you are entering to take possession of it. [6] Observe them carefully, for this will show your wisdom and understanding to the nations, who will hear about all these decrees and say, "Surely this great nation is a wise and understanding people."*

A house that has all of its subcontractors doing their individual roles becomes a great house that many would want to live in. A house that has contractors competing for the same job or contractors refusing to do their work results in a house that no one wants to live in. The first house will receive praise and recognition for its accomplishment. Christian homes should receive praise and recognition as they are the backbone God uses for a wise and free society.

The roles we are learning about in the family are to help us build a successful society. The family is God's training ground for every role that is needed in an ordered society. Christian families are to be the light the world is looking for to find peace, contentment, and order. Remember, as the family goes so goes the nation.

If you are outside on a rainy day and don't want to get wet, an umbrella is your best tool. Umbrellas keep us dry and out of the hot sun. If you don't open an umbrella for protection in the rain or hot sun, you will get wet or sunburned. The four God-ordained institutions are like umbrellas. They have been created by God to give us protection and to promote order, which in turn gives us peace and contentment. When we submit to God's order, we come under His protection and the plans that he has set out for us.

Self-Government – We are to submit to Christ. *Acts 3:19 (NIV) [19] Repent, then, and turn to God, so that your sins may be wiped out, that times of refreshing may come from the Lord.*

Family Government – Children are to submit to parents. *Colossians 3:20 (NIV)* [20] *Children, obey your parents in everything, for this pleases the Lord.*

Church Government – We are to submit to our church leaders. *Hebrews 13:17 (NIV)* [17] *Obey your leaders and submit to their authority. They keep watch over you as men who must give an account. Obey them so that their work will be a joy, not a burden, for that would be of no advantage to you.*

Civil Government – We are to submit to our governing authorities. *Romans 13:1 (NIV)* [1] *Everyone must submit himself to the governing authorities, for there is no authority except that which God has established. The authorities that exist have been established by God.* When a parent gives instruction to a child, the child needs to submit to their authority, so that it may go well with them. For example: The parent tells the toddler not to touch the stove because it is hot. If the child rebels against authority and touches the stove, they will get burned. In this situation, it is obvious that the child should obey authority, but there are other factors as well.

The greatest factor is God and His watchful eye. **God keeps a record of all things** *2 Corinthians 5:10 (NIV)* [10] *For we must all appear before the judgment seat of Christ, that each one may receive what is due him for the things done while in the body, whether good or bad.* **God watches all things and He rewards those who obey Him.** *Deuteronomy 28:2 (NIV)* [2] *All* *these blessings will come upon you and accompany you if you obey the LORD your God:* **He also curses those who do not obey Him.** *Deuteronomy 28:15 (NIV)* [15] *However, if you do not obey the LORD your God and do not carefully follow all his commands and decrees I am giving you today, all these curses will come upon you and overtake you:*

Children are called to obey and honor their parents. *Ephesians 6:1-3 (NIV)* [1] *Children,* **obey** *your parents in the Lord, for this is right.* [2] *"***Honor** *your father and mother"–which is the first commandment with a promise- -* [3] *"that it may go well with you and that you may enjoy long life on the earth."* This passage reinstates the promise of a blessing from the Ten Commandments for those who will obey. This is the fifth commandment of the Ten Commandments.

Disobedience is easier to see than obedience because disobedience brings confusion, strife, contention, and disorder. If a teacher is trying to instruct children and there is disorder, it will be seen clearly. However, when there is order, life is pleasant and everything is in place. In the Self-Government institution, we learned that we are created to serve. Servants are to listen attentively to fulfill the expectations of the authorities that are over them.

The opposite of honor is shame. It is the parent's responsibility to teach their children to obey authority. Children who obey authority bring honor to the parents. Children who disobey authority bring

82

shame to the parents. *Proverbs 10:1 (NIV) [1] The proverbs of Solomon: A wise son brings joy to his father, but a foolish son grief to his mother. Proverbs 17:25 (NIV) [25] A foolish son brings grief to his father and bitterness to the one who bore him. Proverbs 19:26 (NIV) [26] He who robs his father and drives out his mother is a son who brings shame and disgrace.*

All of us disobey God and are tempted to go our own way. We learned in a previous Life Truth that we all need a new nature. We need to submit ourselves to God. We need to ask Jesus for the strength to be obedient and bring honor to God by our actions.

When children begin to reason and understand, we need to teach them to look at life from God's playbook. For example: Would your child be honoring you if they begged for the candy bar and threw a fit while you were shopping in a store? Of course not. Children need to hear the expectations that God has for them and understand His desire for them to walk in true obedience. Children need to be aware of their role in the family. As parents we must realize that we are not just teaching children to obey for our benefit, but we are teaching them to obey so that they may become godly citizens in a peaceful and ordered society. We are raising citizens for the heavenly kingdom. *Proverbs 29:17 (NIV) [17] Discipline your son, and **he will give you peace**; he will bring delight to your soul.*

Unfortunately, not all children grow up to obey their parents. Some decide to go their own way and not follow Christ. Others leave the faith and live very selfish lives. Parents need to remain faithful and obey God's plan for raising obedient children. God promises us that when they are grown they will not depart from it.

Here are four Biblical points children need to remember.

1. God's plan is always best

Proverbs 3:5 (NIV) [5] Trust in the LORD with all your heart and lean not on your own understanding;

Galatians 6:7-9 (NIV) [7] Do not be deceived: God cannot be mocked. A man reaps what he sows. [8] The one who sows to please his sinful nature, from that nature will reap destruction; the one who sows to please the Spirit, from the Spirit will reap eternal life.

We must understand that God is the rewarder. Our corrupt nature does not want to submit to authority. Our disobedience inevitably brings consequences. God wants us to be blessed. The authorities He has established are for our benefit. As we submit to God and His plan of authority, we fulfill our roles and we experience His blessings. God not only established the four institutions, but he gave the power to discipline to three of them.

Family Government has the rod. *Proverbs 13:24 (NIV) [24] He who spares the rod hates his son, but he who loves him is careful to discipline him. Proverbs 22:15 (NIV) [15] Folly is bound up in the heart of a child, but the rod of discipline will drive it far from him. Proverbs 23:13 (NIV) [13] Do not withhold discipline from a child; if you punish him with the rod, he will not die. Proverbs 29:15 (NIV) [15] The rod of correction imparts wisdom, but a child left to himself disgraces his mother.*

God chose the family He placed you in. Just as your mom and dad will give an account of how they raised you, you will give an account of what kind of child you have been. Were you obedient? Were you respectful? Did you honor your parents? Did you ask God to get the folly out of you?

Many counselors and psychologists say that it is wrong to spank children. This is one of Satan's tools to destroy a society. If we do not teach children to obey authority at home, eventually they grow up without respecting any authority. Can we not see the rebellion and the lack of respect for authority in our nation? God's design has always been for the family to be the training ground for a godly society. Have some families used the rod in inappropriate ways toward their children? Yes. The Bible tells them not to exasperate their children. However, their improper use of discipline does not negate God's Word and His instruction to use the rod appropriately. The rod is to be used when children are young. Later, as children grow up, other appropriate discipline should be used. (Time outs, lack of privileges, groundings, loss of allowance, more chores, the writing of verses that relate to the rebellion or sin; etc…)

Church Government has excommunication. *I Corinthians 5:4-5 (NIV) [4] When you are assembled in the name of our Lord Jesus and I am with you in spirit, and the power of our Lord Jesus is present, [5] hand this man over to Satan, so that the sinful nature may be destroyed and his spirit saved on the day of the Lord. I Corinthians 5:11-13 (NIV) [11] But now I am writing you that you must not associate with anyone who calls himself a brother but is sexually immoral or greedy, an idolater or a slanderer, a drunkard or a swindler. With such a man do not even eat. [12] What business is it of mine to judge those outside the church? Are you not to judge those inside? [13] God will judge those outside. "Expel the wicked man from among you."*

The church is to bring correct doctrine and instruction to enable parents to do their job at home. It is important to test what the church is saying by what the Word of God says and then obey God's commands.

Civil Government has the sword. *Romans 13:4-5 (NIV) [4] For he is God's servant to do you good. But if you do wrong, be afraid, for he does not bear the sword for nothing. He is God's servant, an agent of wrath to bring punishment on the wrongdoer. [5] Therefore, it is necessary to submit to the authorities, not only because of possible* *punishment but also because of conscience.* Conscience because God will hold us accountable to how we obeyed!

Notice how this passage puts the Lord's discipline and the Governments together. *Proverbs 24:21-22 (NIV)* *[21] Fear the LORD and the king, my son, and do not join with the rebellious, [22] for those two will send sudden destruction upon them, and who knows what calamities they can bring?*

Order in society is a result of obedience to authority.

Obedience equals blessings. God's plan is that you stay away from the rebellious. The rebellious are those who do not want to obey authority. They do not want to obey their parents, teachers, leaders, and adults.

2. Submit even under injustice

Paul was writing to Timothy and giving him instruction on some of the things we need to do as families and churches. *1 Timothy 2:1-4 (NIV)* *[1] I urge, then, first of all, that requests, prayers, intercession and thanksgiving be made for everyone— [2] for kings and all those in authority, that we may live **peaceful and quiet lives in all godliness and holiness.** [3] This is good, and pleases God our Savior, [4] who wants all men to be saved and to come to a knowledge of the truth.*

87

We need to trust God's plan. We need to be praying for the leaders he has established. What if the leaders are ungodly and not leading as Christ would? The Bible says that when we disobey God and His plan, He will give us leaders who will bring us into slavery. God does this to discipline us and to remind us to obey Him. When this happens, we need to repent, ask God to forgive us, and seek the truth in His Word.

The only time Scripture gives permission to disobey authority is when it goes against God's commands. For example, if a government decided to ban Bibles across the land and said that all Bibles needed to be destroyed, this would go against what God would want. We would be innocent in God's eyes if we did not obey this command. We may have to go to prison and suffer the consequences of such an evil government, but our role is to obey God rather than men.

God would expect us to obey in any injustice that does not go directly against his word. *I Peter 2:19-21 (NIV) [19] For it is commendable if a man bears up under the pain of unjust suffering because he is conscious of God. [20] But how is it to your credit if you receive a beating for doing wrong and endure it? But if you suffer for doing good and you endure it, this is commendable before God. [21] To this you were called, because Christ suffered for you, leaving you an example, that you should follow in his steps.*

In the life of Joseph, we see much unjust suffering. We also see him obeying and serving God in the many different trials. This is commendable and what we are called to do. If you think your parents are being too harsh, or other authorities in your life are treating you unjustly or unfairly, you are still called to obey. God is the judge and He will bless you for your obedience during your trials.

Remember the first point. God's plan is always best and He is the rewarder. We must trust God and submit to His authority. If Joseph had been rebellious while he went through his many trials, he would not have been raised to authority. God will raise us up at the proper time when we trust Him!

Galatians 6:7-9 (NIV) [7] *Do not be deceived: God cannot be mocked. A man reaps what he sows.* [8] *The one who sows to please his sinful nature, from that nature will reap destruction; the one who sows to please the Spirit, from the Spirit will reap eternal life.* [9] *Let us not become weary in doing good,* **for at the proper time we will reap a harvest if we do not give up.**

3. Learn the warning signs of rebellion

Our main responsibility is to become like Christ. When we walk in the Spirit with Christ, we walk in peace, joy, and contentment. We walk away from selfishness, pride, and rebellion. We love our neighbors and sow seeds to please the Spirit. How can we know when we are leaving the path of righteousness and leaning toward rebellion? We must remember the opposites from our self-government truths:

Opposite of Servant is to argue and quarrel. (James 4:1-3) – Are you arguing and fighting with others? Servants seek to bless others and not demand their way. If we are fighting, it is a sign that we are not serving others and considering them better than ourselves.

Opposite of Praise is to complain. (Philippians 2:14) – Are you saying things like, *"I don't like this… I don't want to do this… I shouldn't have to… This is not fair…"* God tells us to be thankful in all things. America is the most blessed nation on earth and yet we are seldom satisfied and content. *"I don't like this… or I don't like that… or I don't want to go there… or this is no fun."* Phrases like this reveal a heart that is not seeking to praise God or give Him glory but rather a heart that is selfishly seeking to please the flesh. Many children in this generation think that the church should meet their need to be entertained. We have allowed this by raising *the spoiled* and not *the servants* in our consumer society. Families should attend church to worship God and serve one another.

Opposite of Encouraging is to be a faultfinder. (Ephesians 4:29) – Pointing out the faults and failures of others is not what God commands us to do. We are not to go around bringing up ways in which people offend us, but we are to be giving them courage to succeed in righteousness. Talking about the failures of others or how someone offended us is gossip. We should be complimenting the good things people are doing and encouraging them to continue in the faith. We should come alongside them and help supply what they're lacking, in order for them to conquer whatever holding them back.

Opposite of Witnessing is being silent about Jesus. (Philemon 1:6) – When we are not sharing our faith in God with others, we are being silent. Silence reveals that we are more concerned with what others think of us than what God thinks of us. God is continually blessing us and we should be faithfully telling others of all of His good works! Not acknowledging God to others is a sign of self-pride and the false belief that we can sustain our own lives.

Opposite of being holy is being worldly. (2 Corinthians 6:14 -7:1) – What type of friends are you hanging out with? Do they want to please God? Are they doing things that would go against the commands of God? It is so important to realize the dangers of being influenced to do evil. All of us have corrupt natures and desire to do things that go against the Scriptures. God's Word tells us to avoid bad company and to seek to be with those who will influence us to obey God. What type of media are you allowing into your temple? Are they things that glorify God or things that glorify the world? We must be careful to seek holiness in all we do, just as the Bible says.

4. Become leaders not consumers

If you did a search for the most and least trusted professions, you would have similar results on both lists. Somewhere near the top of the most trusted list would be nurses and firemen. The bottom of the least trusted list would be car salesmen and politicians.

Many parents hope that their child chooses to be a doctor or lawyer when they grow up. Most want this for their child because of the monetary income that they would most likely make. Is it wrong for parents to wish for their children to be secure financially? It could be.

Our goal is to understand that God created us and has a special purpose for each and every one of us. Our purpose is not to be consumers but to be His leaders on this earth. A consumer is one that consumes. In America, there is much to consume: new houses, cars, boats, RV's, ATV's, guns, shoes, clothes, food, video games, phones, and so much more. Are these things in and of themselves evil? No. But if we are not using them for God and His glory, then yes. Our ultimate goal is to be preparing for heaven. It is not to make ourselves comfortable here on this earth.

Look at what Jesus said in *Mark 8:34-36 (NIV)* [34] *Then he called the crowd to him along with his disciples and said: "If anyone would come after me, he must deny himself and take up his cross and follow me.* ³⁵ *For whoever wants to save his life will lose it, but whoever loses his life for me and for the gospel will save it.* ³⁶ *What good is it for a man to gain the whole world, yet forfeit his soul?*

When we look at the bottom of the least trusted professions and see politicians, many parents think, *"We don't want our child to be a politician."* It is easy to see their point. No one wants their child to be labeled in a least trusted profession; but when we have the least trusted leading us where are we headed?

How awesome would it be to have the most trusted leading our nation into righteousness? Shouldn't we want to have people of great integrity making decisions based upon the future of our nation?

If the least trusted are in office now what will our nation be like in another 50 years? Christians are to be raising the righteous to lead in society. We need Christian politicians, ministers, missionaries, businessmen, policemen, factory workers, janitors, doctors, lawyers, and everything else. Our commission is to be teaching society how to follow Jesus and be blessed by Him. Our goal in life is not to sit back and be consumers, but to engage society with the gospel and lead in the areas of righteousness.

We need Debras who will judge in the land. We need men like Solomon, Moses, and Joshua who will rule the nation with righteousness. We need doctors, like Luke, who will not only help people with medicine, but with the gospel. We need Pauls, who will go on missionary journeys teaching people how to govern their lives by God's Word. We need people like Erastus who will be on the city council and rule righteously. (Romans 16:23) History says that he not only was on the city council but that he used his own money to help the city. That is a Godly politician. Instead of raising taxes, he paid for something out of his own pocket.

Our focus needs to turn away from our comforts and entertainment. We need to turn toward Christ and build His kingdom here upon the earth. *Matthew 6:9-10 (NIV)[9] "This, then, is how you should pray: "'Our Father in heaven, hallowed be your name, [10] your kingdom come, your will be done on earth as it is in heaven.* We need to be longing for our heavenly home while engaging this society with the truth of God's Word. To engage them means that we are going to need to know the Bible and know it well. We cannot teach them what we do not know.

What do we know and love? What does our energy and money go toward in America? Entertainment. We are consumers and not leaders. What is the best way to realize this? Look at who makes the most in our society: actors, athletes, technology-based companies, and pop chart musicians. We are so busy taking our kids to so many different activities that we have no time to train them to be the righteous in society. We are to be training them daily for their future responsibilities in the world. We must turn away from this consumer mentality and start raising the righteous to lead the nation. Our children may never be politicians, but they need to know what God requires of politicians. How can they vote correctly if they don't know what God expects? We have so many things out of order in our society. Civil Government is fulfilling church government responsibilities. Family government is failing in multiple responsibilities. We have strayed from God's order and His divine plans for our society. We need to re-learn our responsibilities and get back to His design for our lives.

We need to be investing our time and energy into learning the Scriptures and then teaching others the ways of God. We need to be raising righteous children who will become leaders and not just consumers.

Once we realize that our purpose is to know God and make him known among the nations, we will focus more of our attention on His Word. Righteous leaders will produce harmony in a society. We have a rise in evil today due to our consumer mentality and our lack of fulfilling God's design for our lives as leaders of society. We would rather let someone else worry about the problems in government, education, welfare, DFS, national debt, abortion, homosexuality, gambling, pornography, sex trafficking, greed, child abuse, drugs, and on and on. We must make time for the discipline necessary to train up a child in the instruction of the Lord. **We must raise leaders for the future of America.** We need those who are willing to go into government and speak up for God's Word. We need those who are willing to go door-to-door telling their neighbors about following Christ. We need those who will be on the city council, school board, or mayors of their town to teach about righteousness. We need those who will begin a Bible study at work teaching others about God's Word and His institutions. We need those who will invite at least one family into their home to study the God-ordained institutions. We need those who will begin a Bible Study in a low-income apartment complex teaching them the ways of God. God has a purpose for us in this generation. Our purpose is to call this nation to repent. We have a purpose just like Esther did during her generation. This is what Mordecai told Esther. *Esther 4:14 (NIV)* [14] *For if you remain silent at this time, relief and deliverance for the Jews will arise from another place, but you and your father's family will perish. And who knows but that you have come to royal position for such a time as this?"*

We need to begin suffering for the good and engaging our culture with the truth. We need to be leaders and not just consumers. **Are your children equipped to lead in society and teach the nation God's commands? Are they ready to be examples of obedience in society?**

WORKSHEET FOR FAMILY GOVERNMENT
LIFE TRUTH # 4
CHILDREN'S RESPONSIBILITIES

Question: What is God's design for children?
Answer: God's design for a child is to know Christ, obey authority and grow up to lead in society.

Ephesians 6:1-3 (NIV) [1] Children, obey your parents in the Lord, for this is right. [2] "Honor your father and mother"– which is the first commandment with a promise– [3] "that it may go well with you and that you may enjoy long life on the earth."

> Write out the Life Truth, question, and answer on one side of an index card and the verse on the other side. Keep it in your Bible for the week. Work on it every day individually and as a family. Have it memorized by next week.

From our memory verse we learn that children are called to obey and honor their parents. Read Matthew 21:28-32. Is obedience more than just saying that we will obey?

Read John 14:15-24. If we love God what will we do?

Read Exodus 20:12. What commandment is this? Who is telling us to obey our parents?

Honor is more than just liking someone. It is to esteem and treat them with great respect.

Circle the things that would be honoring to your parents:

- Rolling your eyes
- Doing what you are told to do.
- Looking for ways to help around the house .
- Cleaning your room even when not asked.
- Reading your Bible
- Speaking kindly to people you meet
- Playing nice with your siblings.
- Complaining about dinner.

Write down one negative way and one positive way to honor your parents.

Read Proverbs 20:11. What can people tell about us in our actions?
Was this obedience immediate or were they hesitant to obey?

Read Matthew 4:18-22.   Read
Exodus 3:10-4:17.
Read Genesis 19:12-26. What did Lot's wife do wrong?
Why is it important to follow God's Word carefully?

Based on this LIFE TRUTH what commitments do you need to make to help children be all that God has called them to be? What commitments will you make this week as a family?

FAMILY-GOVERNMENT LIFE TRUTH # 5
A FAMILY IS RESPONSIBLE
TO GET RID OF ANGER

We have already learned that one of the main responsibilities in the family is to raise the righteous. The main training ground for fulfilling such a task begins in the home, as parents seek to bring their children up in the training and instruction of the Lord.

Adam and Eve, the very first family, had an anger issue that all families can relate to. Although, most families do not ever experience the tragedy of murder that stemmed from Cain's jealously and anger, we have all dealt with anger in our families on some level. (Genesis 4)

In the Sermon on the Mount in Matthew, Chapter 5, Jesus elevated the sin of being angry with our brother to that of being a murderer. So while we may not actually carry out the act of murder, the issue of our heart is the same and deserving of the same judgment as a murderer.

Anger is not always sin. Jesus got angry. *Mark 3:5 (NIV)* [5] *He looked around at them in anger and, deeply distressed at their stubborn hearts, said to the man, "Stretch out your hand." He stretched it out, and his hand was completely restored.*

Righteous anger occurs when we are defending the name of God or are fighting against a Biblical injustice of others. Most of the time our anger is not because we are standing up for God or others. We are usually angry because things are not going the way we think they should. This is considered man's anger and not righteous indignation from God. Notice what James says in *James 1:19-20 (NIV)* [19] *My dear brothers, take note of this: Everyone should be quick to listen, slow to speak and slow to become angry,* [20] *for* **man's anger** *does not bring about the righteous life that God desires.* Human anger is rooted in pride and does not bring about the righteous life that God intends for His people. The Bible also says in, *Ephesians 4:26 (NIV)* [26] *"In your anger do not sin":* As humans, we will get angry and we will desire to explode in our anger, but the Scriptures command us not to sin in our anger. In fact, the Scriptures tell us to get rid of it. *Ephesians 4:31-32 (NIV)* [31] *Get rid of* **all** *bitterness, rage* and anger, *brawling and slander, along with every form of malice.* Our human anger is part of the old nature that must be crucified.

All of us have done things in anger. We have regretted our actions, words, and even our thoughts during angry outbursts. **Many times angry people come from angry families and the stronghold is passed down from generation to generation.** Have you ever regretted your angry outburst and then made a bold statement like, *"That's it! I am never going to get angry again!"* Guess what? You will get angry again. The problem with that statement is that you cannot control your angry feelings. **The main issue is how will you control yourself when those emotions arise? What can you do to help overcome your angry outbursts? How can you break the stronghold in your life?** Thankfully, the Scriptures give us insight into how we can deal with, understand, and overcome our anger.

Anger is a natural response. It sometimes gives us the energy we need to fight against an injustice or to stand up for God. However, anger can cause us trouble when we use it for our own glory or our own satisfaction.

We cannot fulfill God's command to love one another if we are angry. When we are angry we can be harsh, grind our teeth, say hurtful words, throw things, hit, glare with our eyes, and even yell. The list can go on and on.

Our natural response to any sin is to justify it. With our anger we may say phrases like:
- *"Well, not all anger is sin."*
- *"That's the only way I can get their attention."*
- *"If they had not acted that way I would not have had to respond like I did."*
- *"They deserved it."*

Human anger is a sin. It is a good indicator that something else is wrong. Anger is like a warning light on the dashboard of our heart.

When the check engine light goes on in our car, we know that we should check the engine and take care of the issue. If we do not take care of the issue, it will turn into a bigger problem. The same is true with our anger. When we are getting angry, we need to stop and check our heart to make sure it is in the right condition. Are you getting easily upset? Are you impatient with others? Are you harsh or short when people try to speak with you? Are people getting on your nerves?

Remember what Jesus said about the mouth. *Matthew 12:34 (NIV) ³ ... For out of the overflow of the heart the mouth speaks.* When we have outburst of anger, and we say mean and hurtful things, it is an issue of our heart. If we have outbursts often, we could have a stronghold in our heart that results in anger. Many times this stronghold is an issue of rebellion, hidden sin, un-forgiveness or pride. Let's look at some of the Biblical warning lights for anger.

ANGER CAN BE A WARNING LIGHT FOR:

1. REBELLION

The very first murder is recorded in *Genesis 4:3-12 (NIV) ³ In the course of time Cain brought some of the fruits of the soil as an offering to the LORD. ⁴ But Abel brought fat portions from some of the firstborn of his flock. The LORD looked with favor on Abel and his offering, ⁵ but on Cain and his offering he did not look with favor. So Cain was very angry, and his face was downcast.* ⁶ *Then the LORD said to Cain, "Why are you angry? Why is your face downcast?* ⁷ *If you do what is right, will you not be accepted? But if you do not do what is right, sin is crouching at your door; it desires to have you, but you must master it."* ⁸ *Now Cain said to his brother Abel, "Let's go out to the field." And while they were in the field, Cain attacked his brother Abel and killed him.* ⁹ *Then the LORD said to Cain, "Where is your brother Abel?" "I don't know," he replied. "Am I my brother's keeper?"* ¹⁰ *The LORD said, "What have you done? Listen! Your brother's blood cries out to me from the ground.* ¹¹ *Now you are under a curse and driven from the ground, which opened its mouth to receive your brother's blood from your hand.* ¹² *When you work the ground, it will no longer yield its crops for you. You will be a restless wanderer on the earth."*

Cain was the firstborn to Adam and Abel was his younger brother. From this passage, we learn that Cain brought "some of the fruits" of the soil as an offering to the Lord. However, when we do not bring an offering to God that pleases Him, it is sin. We learn in the first book of the Bible that God desires for us to bring Him the "first fruits" or the best that we have been given. This shows God that we understand who He is and that we are thankful to Him for providing for all of our needs.

Abel brought fat portions from the firstborn of his flock. These two young brothers had learned that they needed to bring offerings to the Lord because Adam and Eve had been their example. God had instructed Adam to train his children in this way. Cain had seen his father bring in the first fruits and the best from God's provisions, but he decided not to follow his parents' example. Abel, on the other hand, loved God and wanted to please him. As the offerings were brought before the Lord, the Lord looked with favor upon Abel's offerings, but not on Cain's. Cain, because of his rebellion and defiance to obey God, became very angry.

The Lord spoke to Cain and gave him advice to help him deal with his anger. *Genesis 4:6-7 (NIV)* [6] *Then the LORD said to Cain, "Why are you angry? Why is your face downcast?* [7] *If you do what is right, will you not be accepted? But if you do not do what is right, sin is crouching at your door; it desires to have you, but you must master it."* At this point, Cain could have cried out to the Lord for help. Instead, Cain in his rebellion toward God, displayed uncontrollable hatred for his own brother.

Cain killed his younger brother who was just obeying God. If we are angry at someone, we need to ask ourselves, *"Are we angry because they are obeying God and we are not?* When we are rebelling against God, many times the people we get angry at the most are the ones who are obeying God. We behave this way because their obedient lifestyle convicts us. *I John 3:12 (NIV)* [12] *Do not be like Cain, who belonged to the evil one and murdered his brother. And why did he murder him? Because his own actions were evil and his brother's were righteous.*

104

Have you ever heard someone say, *"They only thing that the church wants is money."* Or perhaps they say, *"Every time I go to church the preacher preaches about money."* What is this anger revealing? It is revealing a rebellion toward God and an unwillingness to bring in the offering that God requires. Does God need the offering? Will He struggle if we do not bring it in? Of course not! God is using our offerings to remind us of who He is and how we need to be thankful for what He has provided for us.

As a father, I may see a man who is spending quality time with his family while I am a workaholic. I may justify my work load and say things like, *"If I had an easy job I could spend more time with my family as well. "* The truth is that life choices often convict us. Deep down we all know that we should be spending quality time raising our children.

Perhaps you're a wife who sees another woman managing her home well. She is able to keep things in order, is helping to raise the righteous, and has joy in her heart. This may convict you and make you angry. You may say things like, *"Well, if I stayed home all the time I could do that as well."* You feel convicted because you know that one of the wife's main responsibilities is to manage the home.

Most of the time, the anger in our heart erupts in the family. We are harsh because we feel convicted about certain areas in our lives. We may be short-tempered, yell, or give the silent treatment to members of our family because we are rebelling against God in some area. When the warning light goes on, we need to check the condition of our heart and repent of our rebellion.

Cain's rebellion was passed down from generation to generation. We see this clearly in his descendant Lamach. After Cain was cursed by God because of his sin, he still did not repent. The Bible says he married a woman and started a family. In the seventh generation, we see the continuance of rebellion when Lamach married two women, going against God's design of one man and one woman. *Genesis 4:19 (NIV)* *¹⁹ Lamech married two women, one named Adah and the other Zillah.* In his rebellion he makes a bold statement of the hatred that was in him. *Genesis 4:23-24 (NIV) ²³ Lamech said to his wives, "Adah and Zillah, listen to me; wives of Lamech, hear my words. I have killed a man for wounding me, a young man for injuring me. ²⁴ If Cain is avenged seven times, then Lamech seventy-seven times."* Lamech was an angry man who was living in rebellion towards God.

The words of our mouth reveal the issues of the heart. When mean hurtful words come out of our mouths, we need to reflect upon our own spiritual lives to make sure that we are right with God. *Proverbs 10:11 (NIV) ¹¹ The mouth of the righteous is a fountain of life, but violence overwhelms the mouth of the wicked.*

When the warning light of anger turns on, we need to search our hearts and make sure we are not rebelling against God in some area.

2. HIDDEN SIN

King David was a believer who sinned, but instead of confessing his sin and making things right, he tried to hide his sin. His first sin was not going to war with his men. *2 Samuel 11:1 (NIV)* [1] *In the spring, at the time* _when kings go off to war,_ *David sent Joab out with the king's men and the whole Israelite army. They destroyed the Ammonites and besieged Rabbah. But* _David_ _remained in Jerusalem._ David should have been at war with his men. Instead he stayed home and committed adultery with Bathsheba. This would not have happened had he been where he was supposed to be. Often Christians think that it is no big deal to miss church or skip a quiet time or two, but this lack of spiritual preparation opens them up for the enemy's attacks.

After King David learned that Bathsheba was pregnant, he attempted to hide his sin by having her husband return home to be with her. When Uriah, Bathsheba's husband, would not spend time with his wife, for the honor of his fighting soldiers, David went a step further and had him killed in battle. The plan was to make it look like an accident. A few men knew what the king was doing and obeyed the evil plan anyway. (2 Samuel 11)

God sent Nathan the prophet to open the eyes of David and reveal to him his sin. *2 Samuel 12:1-6 (NIV)* *¹ The LORD sent Nathan to David. When he came to him, he said, "There were two men in a certain town, one rich and the other poor. ² The rich man had a very large number of sheep and cattle, ³ but the poor man had nothing except one little ewe lamb he had bought. He raised it, and it grew up with him and his children. It shared his food, drank from his cup and even slept in his arms. It was like a daughter to him. ⁴ "Now a traveler came to the rich man, but the rich man refrained from taking one of his own sheep or cattle to prepare a meal for the traveler who had come to him. Instead, he took the ewe lamb that belonged to the poor man and prepared it for the one who had come to him." ⁵ David burned with anger against the man and said to Nathan, "As surely as the LORD lives, the man who did this deserves to die! ⁶ He must pay for that lamb four times over, because he did such a thing and had no pity."*

The Bible says that David burned with anger against the man. The sin that Nathan spoke of was similar to the sin that David had committed. Old Testament law stated that the rich man should repay the poor man four times over. But David went beyond what the law stated and said that the rich man deserved to die and should be shown no pity. It was the hidden sin in David's life that produced in him such anger toward others.

So another warning light is hidden sin. We can openly rebel against God which leads us to anger or we can hide the sin in our lives and display even more anger toward others. In both cases, our hearts are revealed by what is coming out of our mouths. David spoke harshly about the man who had sinned. He spoke in anger and not in love. We need God to pour His love into our hearts in order for us to pass that love on to others. When we hide sin from God, our hearts become corrupted and our mouths reveal the sin. People that are hiding adultery, pornography, gambling, drugs, alcohol, and other similar sins of the flesh, become angry at others and lash out from their hearts. The family is often the recipient of their sinful words.

If you are the one hiding sin, it is vital that you repent and turn to God. *Galatians 5:19-21 (NIV) [19] The acts of the sinful nature are obvious: sexual immorality, impurity and debauchery; [20] idolatry and witchcraft; hatred, discord, jealousy, fits of rage, selfish ambition, dissensions, factions [21] and envy; drunkenness, orgies, and the like. I warn you, as I did before, that those who live like this will not inherit the kingdom of God.*

Did you notice God's grace in the life of Cain and David? The Lord spoke to Cain and sought to help him before he committed murder. The Lord pronounced the curse and judgment upon Cain for his disobedience and yet Cain did not cry out for mercy. In David's life, God sent a prophet to speak to him and reach out to him in order for David to confess and repent of his sin. If David had not confessed and repented of his sins, he would not have been allowed into heaven. God's love reaches out to us. He longs to forgive, to restore, and to heal our hearts so that our anger does not come out and hurt others. We need God's mercy and grace in our lives. Instead of hiding our sin, we need to run to God and beg for His forgiveness.

3. PRIDE

Pride is an undo confidence in yourself. Many times pride can produce anger because you think life should go a certain way and when it doesn't you get upset. When people begin to behave in a way that affects you and your plans, you become frustrated.

Just recently, I was on my way home from a church camp with my family and we pulled into a gas station to get diesel. There was only one island that had diesel and both of the lanes were full. As I looked at the vehicles, I noticed that neither car was filling up and both cars were empty. As I waited and waited and waited, I began to get irritated (which is a nicer word than angry). I began to voice my frustration and my oldest daughter overheard me. Some friends called her on her cell phone and my daughter began to explain to them that I was frustrated at the cars. At that point, I was not only irritated at the cars, but I was also irritated at my daughter for portraying me in a negative light. This is pride! Pride can produce anger.

Did you know that, as Christians, our anger can be controlled? Just think about how many times children can make parents upset when they are trying to get to church and no one is cooperating. There can be many outbursts of anger just on the way to church. But what happens to the parent who was yelling at the kids in the car when they enter church? The big smile and the "everything is fine look" miraculously comes over them. Or when you are yelling at the family at home and the phone rings. How do you answer? You answer with a loving "Hello".

When we get angry in our pride, we must search our hearts and learn to allow the Holy Spirit to live through us. The Bible says in *Psalm 4:4 (NIV)* [4] *In your anger do not sin; when you are on your beds, search your hearts and be silent.* We need to be searching our hearts and asking God to reveal the rebellion, hidden sin, un-forgiveness or pride that is causing our anger.

As parents, we have great expectations for our children. We expect them to come out of the womb saying, "Yes, *sir*" and "Yes, *ma'am*." We expect them to be very polite and respectful to everyone they meet. We expect them to never thrown temper tantrums or whine. Is this realistic? The first child ever born was Cain and he killed his brother. Children enter the world with a corrupt nature. They enter the world being selfish, self-centered, and prideful. Their first word is usually, "*Mine, mine, mine.*"

It is the parent's job to point them to God and teach them that without Christ they cannot obey or please God. Children must be taught that we are all sinners in need of Jesus's salvation. They need to understand that we receive salvation from our sins by making Jesus our Lord. Parents are to teach their children how to pray, repent, and follow Him.

When the issues of child-rearing arise, we should stay calm and realize that this is a job God has asked us to do. If children came out perfect, God would not be asking us to train them. I speak somewhat sarcastically, but I hope that you are getting the point. We get upset many times in the family because our kids are embarrassing us and not meeting our expectations. We get upset when our goals are not getting accomplished and our children are not fulfilling what we want them to do. We must come to the realization that every day is the Lord's and we are simply His servants.

Is it godly to set goals and live a disciplined life? Very much so! But the days are the Lord's and He is the one in control. So when the day does not go as we planned, we must keep a Christ-like attitude and speak as Jesus would, especially to those within our own household.

The family is the training ground for getting rid of our human anger and walking in the Spirit.. The family is to teach it's members how to get rid of the anger.

This is only possibly through Christ, so the church should be a shining light in this area.

There is a story in Luke that tells of Jesus sleeping in a boat when a great storm arises. The storm is so sudden and powerful that it scares the trained fishermen. They are so afraid that they wake up Jesus and tell him that they are going to drown!
Luke 8:22-25 (NIV) ^{22} *One day Jesus said to his disciples, "Let's go over to the other side of the lake." So they got into a boat and set out.* ^{23} *As they sailed, he fell asleep. A squall came down on the lake, so that the boat was being swamped, and they were in great danger.* ^{24} *The disciples went and woke him, saying, "Master, Master, we're going to drown!" He got up and rebuked the wind and the raging waters; the storm subsided, and all was calm.* ^{25} *"Where is your faith?" he asked his disciples. In fear and amazement they asked one another, "Who is this? He commands even the winds and the water, and they obey him."*

Who asked the disciples to get into the boat and go over to the other side? Jesus did. Who knew that the storm would arise while they were in the boat and on the lake? Jesus did. The storm, the timing, the situation; Jesus was not surprised by any of it.

When situations arise in life that cause us to be afraid or to get angry, we need to remember that this is not a surprise to God. He expects us to call upon Him for help and to trust that He knows what he is doing. We need to have

113

faith that God will help us through the storm. We need to have faith that Jesus can calm the storms of life. Jesus wants us to remain faithful and have a Christ-like attitude as we journey through life. God is more concerned about our character than our goals and comforts.

The warning light of pride is anger. We need to be asking ourselves tough questions as parents. *Am I upset because they are not doing what I want them to do? Am I upset because I do not want to take the time to train them? Am I upset because they are making me look bad as a parent?*

We are commanded to speak encouraging words that build others up and this definitely includes our children. If we are saying demeaning, cutting, or belittling remarks to our children, we are not being obedient to the Word. The Word of God, not our own negative comments, should be used to teach and train our children. *Ephesians 4:29 (NIV)* [29] *Do not let any unwholesome talk come out of your mouths, but only what is helpful for building others up according to their needs, that it may benefit those who listen.*

If you are having a hard time being an encourager, I would suggest that you review Self-Government Life Truth # 6: I AM CREATED TO ENCOURAGE.

WHAT CAN I DO TO OVERCOME MY ANGER?

1. CONFESS YOUR SIN

When Nathan confronted David about his hidden sin, David repented. Nathan pointed out that David was the man! He goes on to pronounce the curse that God is going to give his family because of his sin. After Nathan shares the coming judgment upon David and his family, it says in *2 Samuel 12:13 (NIV)* *13 Then David said to Nathan, "I have sinned against the LORD." Nathan replied, "The LORD has taken away your sin. You are not going to die.* When we repent and confess our sins, God begins to restore and heal. The law required that adulterers and murders be stoned to death, but since David confessed and repented, the punishment was accredited to Christ.

We need to be honest about our anger and confess it as sin. We need to be lying still upon our beds and searching our hearts to see what the warning light is saying. Whether it's rebellion, hidden sin, un-forgiveness or pride, we need to confess and repent. Cain's family was cursed because of his sin. David's family had consequences, but they were lessoned as he repented. Sin brings consequences, not only on ourselves, but many times on our families as well. We have a promise in *1 John 1:9 (NIV)* *9 If we confess our sins, he is faithful and just and will forgive us our sins and purify us from all unrighteousness.*

115

2. FORGIVE THE OFFENDER

The Greek word for stronghold is ochuroma. It means castle or fortress. The Bible tells us specifically in *Ephesians 4:26-27 (NIV)* [26] *"In your anger do not sin":* *Do not let the sun go down while you are still angry,* [27] *and do not give the devil a foothold.* When we do not forgive the offender, we allow a stronghold to enter our lives. The Bible warns us about not dealing with our anger. We are told from the Scriptures to take it seriously and not even go to bed until we have forgiven the offender or dealt with our anger. There are strongholds in people's lives that cause past feelings to arise. When this happens, they get angry and take it out on others. Sometimes they even take the anger out on themselves.

"What makes you angry?" *"What hurts you deeply?"* If a specific situation comes to your mind, there is a very good chance that you have not forgiven the offender. The offender needs to be forgiven, no matter how severe the offense was. You may never be able to have a relationship with that person here on this earth, but the heart must grant forgiveness. Some situations might need a pastor or a Christian counselor to help you through this. If you are having a hard time forgiving, I would suggest that you review Self-Government Life Truth # 8: I AM CREATED TO FORGIVE.

The offender could even be you. You may not have forgiven yourself and allowed the grace of God to

116

empower you and give you peace from the situation. If the offender is you, Hebrews explains what to do. *Hebrews 10:19-23 (NIV)* ¹⁹ *Therefore, brothers, since we have confidence to enter the Most Holy Place by the blood of Jesus,* ²⁰ *by a new and living way opened for us through the curtain, that is, his body,* ²¹ *and since we have a great priest over the house of God,* ²² *let us draw near to God with a sincere heart in full assurance of faith, having our hearts sprinkled* **to cleanse us from a guilty conscience** *and having our bodies washed with pure water.* ²³ *Let us hold unswervingly to the hope we profess, for he who promised is faithful.* Go boldly to God and seek His forgiveness and experience His mercy and grace. Many times we are too ashamed to go to God, but this is what all of us need. We need to pray and ask God to forgive us. We need to confess our sins. We need Jesus!

You may have a stronghold passed down to you from generation to generation. You may have been raised with a critical parent. Words to build you up were seldom said, but many words were said to tear you down.

Every one of us desires to hear the words, *"Well done."* We long to hear these words from our parents, but many times the generational sin of faultfinding is passed down. We do not get to experience the power of blessing another. We need to forgive our parents of any negative words, actions, or comments. We need to break the cycle in our generation and pass on the power of blessing one another.

As parents, we need to understand that we are sowing and watering the seed. Many times, we expect our kids to get spiritual truth the first time we instruct them or the first time we train them. Spiritual truth is revealed by the Spirit of God. Our job is to pray for our kids, instruct and train them, and then wait for the harvest of righteousness. Don't fall into the trap that your children will get it the first one hundred times you tell them. Keep training them in love and pray for the harvest. When they finally get the spiritual truth and begin to live in righteousness, rejoice that God revealed it to them!

Sometimes we are so mad at the offender that the stronghold is firm. We must cry out to God in order to be free. It may take us a while, but God's grace will free us from the bondage of un-forgiveness. It is God who judges. We are commanded to love.

Romans 12:17-21 (NIV) [17] *Do not repay anyone evil for evil. Be careful to do what is right in the eyes of everybody.* [18] *If it is possible, as far as it depends on you, live at peace with everyone.* [19] *Do not take revenge, my friends, but leave room for God's wrath, for it is written: "It is mine to avenge; I will repay," says the Lord.* [20] *On the contrary: "If your enemy is hungry, feed him; if he is thirsty, give him something to drink. In doing this, you will heap burning coals on his head."* [21] *Do not be overcome by evil, but overcome evil with good.*

3. **MAKE RESTITUTION**

Have you been easily upset? Have you said hurtful, belittling, or negative words? After you have made it right with God and dealt with your rebellion, hidden sin, un-forgiveness or pride, then it is time to make restitution with those whom you have offended.

There is a story in the Bible about Zacchaeus, a greedy tax collector who cheated people out of their money. Jesus went to his house and showed this guilty man love and forgiveness. Zacchaeus received God's grace and repented of his sinful ways.

Luke 19:8 (NIV) [8] But Zacchaeus stood up and said to the Lord, "Look, Lord! Here and now I give half of my possessions to the poor, and if I have cheated anybody out of anything, I will pay back four times the amount."

Zacchaeus gave half of his wealth to the poor and then he paid back four times what he cheated people out of. Paying back what he had stolen is called restitution. Most of the time, our anger is expressed in hurtful words. Words the Bible refers to as *tearing down.*

When we do this, we need to go to those we have offended and ask for their forgiveness. Parents need to teach their children how to go to God and then make restitution to those they have offended. This is how we love one another. This is how we heal wounds in the family and restore love and unity.

Parents need to focus on saying words that build their children up. If you have said one word that is negative, be like Zaccahaeus and pay them back four times. Try saying four words or phrases that will bless them. We are to be the light of the world and light represents goodness, kindness, and love. Look at what the Scriptures say about words.

Proverbs 18:20-21 (NIV) [20] From the fruit of his mouth a man's stomach is filled; with the harvest from his lips he is satisfied. [21] The tongue has the power of life and death, and those who love it will eat its fruit.

Asking for forgiveness can bring great healing to a family and restore relationships that have been wounded. Let's walk in peace, joy, and love. Let's show the world how to get rid of human anger.

WORKSHEET FOR FAMILY GOVERNMENT LIFE TRUTH # 5 THE FAMILY IS RESPONSIBLE TO GET RID OF ANGER

Question: What are we to do with anger?
Answer: Our responsibility is to get rid of man's anger and be kind to one another.

Ephesians 4:31-32 (NIV) [31] *Get rid of all bitterness, rage and anger, brawling and slander, along with every form of malice.* [32] *Be kind and compassionate to one another, forgiving each other, just as in Christ God forgave you.*

> Write out the Life Truth, question, and answer on one side of an index card and the verse on the other side. Keep it in your Bible for the week. Work on it every day individually and as a family. Have it memorized by next week.

According to Ephesians we are to get rid of ALL...
B_____, R_____,
A_____, B_____, S
_____, M_____.
We are to be…. K_____,
C_____, F_____

Read Psalm 37:8. What does this passage tell us to do about anger?   About wrath?

Read 2 Chronicles 26:16-20. Uzziah the king became afflicted by God with what disease?

What two sins was Uzziah guilty of? P_____
and A_____.

Pride causes us to respond in anger. Why was Uzziah
upset?

Pride can cause us to become angry when people are
not responding or behaving as we think they should.
Is it right to yell at someone because they are not
doing what we want them to?

Read I Samuel 18:1-16. The song made Saul
J_____. His pride made him very
A_____. Anger opens us up to the influence
of Satan. What came forcefully upon Saul in vs 10?

Read Ephesians 4:26-27. What gives the devil a
foothold in our life?

***PLEASE DO THIS NEXT PART AT HOME
WITH YOUR FAMILY***
Read Proverbs 18:21

Everyone deals with pride and anger. All of us have
said and done things, in our anger, that we regret. As
a family, it is important to heal the wounds that we
make during these outbursts. Starting with the father,
apologize to those in your family that you have
offended by your anger. Ask them to forgive you.
Each person in the family can apologize to whomever
they have offended. (Parents may need to help direct
the kids to apologize to their brothers or sisters)

Sometimes we offend even when we do not realize it. Ask each one in the family if someone has done something to offend them. If they bring something up, apologize for the hurt, and don't justify what you did or why you did it.

Based on this LIFE TRUTH what commitments do you need to make in the area of family government? What commitments will you make this week as a family?

FAMILY GOVERNMENT
LIFE TRUTH # 6
A FAMILY IS RESPONSIBLE
TO HAVE AN ALTAR

An altar is a place for bringing sacrifices to God. It was the location where the people of God went to make atonement for their sins. Altars were built by people in the Old Testament when they had an encounter with God. Today, families still need an established alter where they gather and meet with God.

Abraham built an altar in *Genesis 12:7 (NIV)* *7 The LORD appeared to Abram and said, "To your offspring I will give this land." So he built an altar there to the LORD, who had appeared to him.* Isaac built an altar to meet with God. The Bible says in *Genesis 26:24,25 (NIV) 24 That night the LORD appeared to him and said, "I am the God of your father Abraham. Do not be afraid, for I am with you; I will bless you and will increase the number of your descendants for the sake of my servant Abraham." 25 Isaac built an altar there and called on the name of the LORD. There he pitched his tent, and there his servants dug a well.*

A family altar is an intentional place and time to focus upon God and to build a relationship with Him as a family. Meditating upon God's Word and talking with our families and others about the goodness of God does not replace the family altar. **Since Christ is**

our atoning sacrifice we no longer need to come together and sacrifice animals, but we do need to come together to confess our sins, seek the Word for knowledge, and make sure that we are remaining reconciled to God and one another.

Many people are wounded in our generation. They are not experiencing the freedom that we have in Christ. There are divorces that could have been healed through a family altar. There are prodigal children who may not have left the faith if their families had been having a family altar. The current divorce rate in the church, plus the number of children who are leaving the faith, is the sad evidence of the lack of families having spiritual encounters with God.

Establishing a family altar can heal many of the offenses that people carry around during their lives. These offenses produce struggles in their relationships. As we talked about in the last Life Truth, many times angry people come from angry families. A person who was wounded by their father may carry around un-forgiveness, which then grows into bitterness, and eventually affects their own marriage. Learning and applying Biblical truths in families heals many wounds that have the potential to destroy families if they're not dealt with.

The Bible does not say, *"Thou shalt have a family altar."* But it does tell us that if we love God, we will obey His teachings. You may already be having a family altar and you just haven't titled it that way; or you may have experienced times with your family that resemble parts of a family altar. The vital piece of this Life Truth is that we must apply these Biblical principles with our own families and teach our children to pass them on to their future families. We must also begin to share these healing principles with others in our hurting world.

Your family will benefit greatly by learning and applying these principles. You may know of a family, a hurting marriage, or friends who could use a family altar to help heal their relationships.

Where should we have a family altar? The place is not as important as the content and the truth that is presented. You could have a family altar in your living room, bedroom, at a park, in your car, or even at your kitchen table. I would encourage you to remove all distractions when you have a family alter. Don't have any cell phones, games, books, magazines, TV's, or anything else that could distract you from God and the truth that is being presented.

What should we do during a family altar? Let's look at some of the principles of a family alter:

1. Read the Bible.

If you have been applying the goals of the Life Truths, your family has already begun to have a family altar. One of the goals of the Life Truths is to read a chapter in the Bible daily as a family. We have already looked at the Biblical command for parents to educate their children in the Word. Deuteronomy 6:4-9 is the reference for this principle.

2. Pray.

Another important aspect is to pray together as a family. Families need to come together and pray for the needs of their family. If your family is in need of income, then ask God together for His provisions. This helps teach your children how to pray. Whatever issue your family may be going through, together you can seek the Lord in prayer (health, finances, relationships, etc…). Children who hear their parents praying learn how to call upon the Lord themselves. If you hear a child who prays well, most likely it is the result of a family who is praying together. It may be uncomfortable for a parent to pray out loud, but it is vital to the spiritual growth of children. You do not have to be eloquent in your words, but you still need to pray out loud as an example for your children. Praying out loud is like learning to ride a bike. It may feel very uncomfortable at first, but soon it will become a very natural thing for you to do.

I Thessalonians 5:17 (NIV) says to *pray continually.* Pray in Jesus name. *John 14:13-14 (NIV) [13] And I will do* **whatever you ask in my name,** *so that the Son may bring glory to the Father. [14]* **You may ask me for anything in my name,** *and I will do it. John 15:16 (NIV) [16] You did not choose me, but I chose you and appointed you to go and bear fruit–fruit that will last. Then the Father will give you* **whatever you ask in my name.**

Some people open in Jesus name and others close in Jesus name. You may start, *"Dear Jesus"* or you may close, *"In Jesus Name, Amen."* **No matter how you pray, just remember how important it is to ask in Jesus name.**

3. Praise.

Singing praises together is something that families should also do. This is a goal every family should work on. You can print off lyrics to hymns and praise songs on the internet and sing them together. You can play a song on the radio or other devices and sing with the music. Review Self Government Life Truth # 5 - I AM CREATED TO PRAISE. This will remind you of the power we have in praise!

We not only need to praise God through song, but also through our words. We need to declare thanks to God when he answers our prayers. We need to praise God when He allows us to go through our trials. Yes, through our trials. We are to be thankful in all things. Hearing a parent say that they are thankful to God when they are going through a hard time educates children and helps them refocus their mindset on God. If God is allowing the trial, then His long range goal is for our benefit, so we can rejoice in all things. *I Thessalonians 5:16-18 (NIV) ¹⁶ Be joyful always; ¹⁷ pray continually; ¹⁸ give thanks in all circumstances, for this is God's will for you in Christ Jesus.*

These three truths are very important to establishing a family altar. The family altar does not need to have a certain length of time and it does not need to be done exactly at the same time every day. The important thing is that families get into the habit of reading the Bible, praying, and praising God together.

We have covered the basic principles to establishing a family altar, but it's also very important to learn about the deeper issues of the heart in family worship time. Fathers, as the leader of your homes, I am calling on you to listen very carefully to this next part about family altars. You are the ones God is expecting to lead your homes in righteousness. If no father is in the home, then the mother should establish these principles during the family altar time.

There are times in our lives when we realize that something is not quite right in the family. Perhaps, the kids are fighting and are mad at one another. Perhaps, a child has a rebellious heart and does not want to submit to God or their parents. Perhaps, spouses are mad at one another and are not speaking to each other.

Women usually discern these issues quicker than men. When they do, they need to be sharing their insights with their husbands. Fathers, when things are not right in the family, God has given you resources to restore unity within the home. It may even be necessary to have a different type of family altar than the traditional one where you read a chapter, praise, and pray.

Notice this passage in *Matthew 5:23-24 (NIV)*
[23] "Therefore, if you are offering your gift at the altar and there remember that your brother has something against you, [24] leave your gift there in front of the altar. First go and be reconciled to your brother; then come and offer your gift.

If we are coming together at the family or the church altar and we realize that something is wrong, we need to stop what we are doing and reconcile the relationship. Christian families need to be obeying the Word and reconciling with others. Look at what Paul said in *2 Corinthians 5:18-19 (NIV): [18] All this is from God, who reconciled us to himself through Christ and gave us the ministry of reconciliation:* As Christians, we have a responsibility to be make sure that we are staying reconciled to God and to one another.

What can I do if I notice division, rebellion, or disunity in my family? Come to Christ and allow Him to heal your hearts. Look at what Peter says in *I Peter 2:24-25 (NIV)* [24] *He himself bore our sins in his body on the tree, so that we might die to sins and live for righteousness;* **by his wounds you have been healed**. We are to go to one another, as Matthew said, and reconcile our relationships. In the worksheet for Family Government # 5, I challenged you to do this exercise.

Everyone deals with pride and anger. All of us have said and done things, in our anger, that we regret. As a family, it is important to heal the wounds that we have caused during these outbursts. The father should start by apologizing to those in his family that he has offended by his anger. He should ask for forgiveness. Each person in the family can then apologize to whomever they have offended as well. (Parents may need to help direct the children to apologize to their brothers or sisters.)

Sometimes we offend even when we do not realize it. Ask each one in the family if someone has done something to offend them. If they bring something up, apologize for the hurt. Don't justify what you did or why you did it.

This restoring of relationships is huge in our society. It is how the church can be the salt and light in our world. If the couple who fought actually came together and asked for forgiveness, they would still be married today. If the son who felt his parents were hypocrites, heard them say they were sorry and asked for his forgiveness, he would still be in the faith today. If the father who was always yelling at his family in anger, came to them and asked for their forgiveness, the anger cycle would have finally been broken.

Here are some important things that you can do during your family altar to heal relationships:

1. HAVE COMMUNION TOGETHER

The Biblical word *communion* means unity and fellowship. We need to be sure our fellowship with God is not broken by sin and that we have unity in our relationships with others. The goal of communion is to make sure that there is unity, forgiveness, and love in our relationships. We need to stop and deal with the issues that arise in life. Everyone gets offended at times. We all do and say things in anger that offend others.

Paul tells the church how we are to be in *Colossians 3:12-14 (NIV)* [12] *Therefore, as God's chosen people, holy and dearly loved, clothe yourselves with compassion, kindness, humility, gentleness and patience.* [13] *Bear with each other and forgive whatever grievances you may have against one another. Forgive as the Lord forgave you.* [14] *And over all these virtues put on love, which binds them all together in perfect unity.*

Notice how Paul tells us to clothe ourselves with Godly qualities. He also tells us to bear with and forgive whatever grievances we may have against one another. Since we are still in our sinful bodies, we fail at times, and therefore need to forgive each other just as God forgives us. God forgives every sin and we need to do the same towards others. This forgiveness is healing and restores the unity in homes.

A great way to establish this healing is to have communion or what many call the Lord's Supper together. I would encourage every family to have communion during their altar time. You do not have to do it every day or every week, but I would encourage every family to do it. Some families have communion once a week, some every quarter, and some whenever they feel like they are drifting apart from God or one another.

We are commanded in the Scriptures to have communion together as a church; but the origin of the Lord's Supper was something that was done in the home. The first communion was done when the nation of Israel was being freed from slavery in Egypt. The Israelites had to place the blood on the door posts. It was called the Passover meal.
The Passover meal is what Jesus was having with the disciples. We also call that meal the Last Supper or the Lord's Supper. Jesus told us to have this supper

until he returns. Just as the church should take the supper together and focus on staying unified in Christ, families need to have this same vision. Where was Jesus having this meal with the disciples? He was having it in a home.

What we learn in our homes is what we bring into the church. If families are establishing forgiveness, unity, and love in the home, it will be evident in the church. What we learn in the home is also what we take with us into society. Since many families are not applying the Biblical principles of being reconciled to God and one another, they are suffering in their relationships in society.

In the New Testament, they would have a meal together and then take the bread and the wine after the meal. While many churches do not practice this aspect of having a meal first, the family could do this during their communion. A family could also take it without having a meal together. In 1 Corinthians, Paul is talking to the church and how they are taking the meal in an unworthy manner. He mentions some of the selfish attitudes they are having in Chapter Eleven. He writes that before they take the supper, they need to be making sure they are right with God. As a father, it is important that you stress and emphasize this truth to your family. You can read the passage in *1 Corinthians 11:27-32 (NIV)* [27] *Therefore, whoever eats the bread or drinks the cup of the Lord in an unworthy manner will be guilty of sinning against the*

body and blood of the Lord. ²⁸ A man ought to examine himself before he eats of the bread and drinks of the cup. ²⁹ For anyone who eats and drinks without recognizing the body of the Lord eats and drinks judgment on himself. ³⁰ That is why many among you are weak and sick, and a number of you have fallen asleep. ³¹ But if we judged ourselves, we would not come under judgment. ³² When we are judged by the Lord, we are being disciplined so that we will not be condemned with the world.
We need to stress that if we do not forgive one another God will not forgive us. *Matthew 6:14-16 (NIV)* ¹⁴ *For if you forgive men when they sin against you, your heavenly Father will also forgive you.* ¹⁵ *But if you do not forgive men their sins, your Father will not forgive your sins..* This would be a great time to review the *get rid of anger* Life Truth verse. *Ephesians 4:31-32 (NIV)* ³¹ *Get rid* **of all** *bitterness, rage and anger, brawling and slander, along with every form of malice.* ³² *Be kind and compassionate to one another,* **forgiving each other, just as in Christ God forgave you.**

Fathers and mothers need to lead their families to get rid of anger and be reconciled to one another before taking communion together. Parents should also emphasize the importance of being right with God before communion is taken.

BIBLICAL STEPS FOR COMMUNION

A. Get right with God

Give everyone time to go to God in prayer and confess their sins to Him. Parents must to teach their children to ask God to reveal to them any sins that they have committed. Then they can confess their sins and repent. Let them know that the Holy Spirit will bring to their mind something that they need to deal with. When the Holy Spirit does, they need to ask Jesus to forgive them. You could encourage them to have a time of silent reflective prayer. Confessing means to agree with God that it is wrong and ask God for His forgiveness. Repent means that they are going to stop committing the sin and head in the other direction of righteousness. This is a great time to remind children that without Christ you cannot obey God and walk in righteousness. You need the help of the Holy Spirit as you ask God for the strength to repent and obey.

B. Get right with one another

Ask the family, *"Did God bring something to your mind that would have been an offense to someone in our family?"* For example: The Holy Spirit convicts a sibling for being too harsh with a younger brother or sister. If God brought this to their mind, they need to ask for forgiveness to the sibling they offended. As parents, we need to be leading this. We need to be asking for forgiveness for the things God is bringing to our minds that have affected those in our family. If a husband was harsh with his wife in front of the kids, he needs to apologize to his wife in front of the kids.

Everyone should be given time to ask if they have offended anyone in the family. Your child may say, *"Dad, when you yelled at me the other day it hurt my feelings."* The dad should respond, *"I am sorry for yelling and hurting your feelings. Will you forgive me?"* Remember, you may have been right in correcting your child, but you sinned if you yelled and did it in anger. Do not justify your behavior, but heal the wound and the offense that your child felt. If you justify why you did what you did, you still have not healed the wound. Your child may not share the next time.

Ask your family if they have an offense against anyone outside of the family. If someone shares something, tell them to pray and ask Jesus to give them the ability to forgive the person for what they have done. Once they have prayed to forgive those who have offended them, take communion together as a family.

Read: *I Corinthians 11:23-24 (NIV)* [23] *For I received from the Lord what I also passed on to you: The Lord Jesus, on the night he was betrayed, took bread,* [24] *and when he had given thanks, he broke it and said, "This is my body, which is for you; do this in remembrance of me."* (Take the bread together.)

Read: *I Corinthians 11:25-26 (NIV)* *25 In the same way, after supper he took the cup, saying, "This cup is the new covenant in my blood; do this, whenever you drink it, in remembrance of me." 26 For whenever you eat this bread and drink this cup, you proclaim the Lord's death until he comes.* (Take the juice together.)

I would encourage you to pray after the supper and thank God for healing your hearts and uniting you together. Remind your family of the character quality of God's love. It says in *I Corinthians 13:5 (NIV) (Love) it keeps no record of wrongs.* The issues that a family brings to the altar need to be sacrificed and brought up no more.

Biblical passages about God's forgiveness that you might read to your family before or after communion are:

I John 1:9 (NIV) 9 If we confess our sins, he is faithful and just and will forgive us our sins and purify us from all unrighteousness.

Isaiah 1:18 (NIV) 18 "Come now, let us reason together," says the LORD. "Though your sins are like scarlet, they shall be as white as snow; though they are red as crimson, they shall be like wool.

Psalm 103:11-13 (NIV) 11 For as high as the heavens are above the earth, so great is his love for those who fear him; 12 as far as the east is from the west, so far has he removed our transgressions from us. 13 As a father has compassion on his children, so the LORD has compassion on those who fear him;

Christian homes have the blood of Jesus to help them forgive and love one another. It is the power that the world is longing for. How many families could have benefited or been saved if they had practiced a family altar time? How many could have been saved if they had shared communion together and forgiven each other? Does your family need healing?

I would encourage you, no matter how old your children are, to begin having a family altar. Perhaps you could invite your grown kids over for a meal and afterwards tell them that you would like to take communion together. Communion is having an intimate relationship with Christ. It is because of our relationship with Christ that we can have an intimate relationship with one another.

Remember we need to be taking communion together to keep the communion in the family.

2. GIVE A PRIESTLY BLESSING

In the Old Testament Moses told Aaron and his sons, who were the priests, to bless the Israelites with a blessing. This is called the priestly blessing.
Numbers 6:22-27 (NIV) [22] *The LORD said to Moses,* [23] *"Tell Aaron and his sons, 'This is how you are to bless the Israelites. Say to them:* [24] *"' "The LORD bless you and keep you;* [25] *the LORD make his face shine upon you and*

be gracious to you; ²⁶ *the LORD turn his face toward you and give you peace."' ²⁷ "So they will put my name on the Israelites, and I will bless them."*

The passage says that the priests are to speak this blessing to the Israelites and God will bless them. The New Testament declares that we are a kingdom of priests. *I Peter 2:9 (NIV) ⁹ But you are a chosen people, a royal priesthood, a holy nation, a people belonging to God.*

We are to be the priests for God and we are to be blessing others, especially those in our own family. In the Old Testament fathers would lay hands on their kids and bless them. Isaac blessed his son Jacob. *Genesis 27:27-29 (NIV) ²⁷ So he (Jacob) went to him and kissed him. When Isaac caught the smell of his clothes, he blessed him and said, "Ah, the smell of my son is like the smell of a field that the LORD has blessed. ²⁸ May God give you of heaven's dew and of earth's richness— an abundance of grain and new wine. ²⁹ May nations serve you and peoples bow down to you. Be lord over your brothers, and may the sons of your mother bow down to you. May those who curse you be cursed and those who bless you be blessed."*

The Bible says that our words have the power of life and death. They can either build up or they can tear down. There is something powerful when we begin to speak priestly blessings over our children and other members of our family. Those who are placed in authority by God should be doing this. Parents we need to be blessing our children.

It does not matter if the one being blessed is deserving of the blessing or acting righteous. The important thing is that the blessing be given. You may have a rebellious child and are wondering how you could bless them? What could you even say?
The blessing is not dependent upon the righteousness of the one receiving it. When Isaac blessed Jacob he was deceiving his father and pretending to be his older brother Esau. *Genesis 27:30-33 (NIV)* ³⁰ *After Isaac finished blessing him and Jacob had scarcely left his father's presence, his brother Esau came in from hunting.* ³¹ *He too prepared some tasty food and brought it to his father. Then he said to him, "My father, sit up and eat some of my game, so that you may give me your blessing."* ³² *His father Isaac asked him, "Who are you?" "I am your son," he answered, "your firstborn, Esau."* ³³ *Isaac trembled violently and said, "Who was it, then, that hunted game and brought it to me? I ate it just before you came and I blessed him—**and indeed he will be blessed!**"*

The passage says, "and indeed he will be blessed!" So the priestly blessing does not depend upon the honor of the one receiving it. Jacob was blessed just as the blessing was stated.

The priestly blessing does not even depend upon the honor of the one giving the blessing. Eli who was a disgraceful priest and a bad father gave a blessing. Eli thought that Hannah, who was praying at the temple, was drunk and he told her to get rid of the wine. *I Samuel 1:15-17 (NIV)* [15] *"Not so, my lord," Hannah replied, "I am a woman who is deeply troubled. I have not been drinking wine or beer; I was pouring out my soul to the LORD.* [16] *Do not take your servant for a wicked woman; I have been praying here out of my great anguish and grief."* [17] *Eli answered, "Go in peace, and **may the God of Israel grant you what you have asked of him**."*

Guess what? God blessed Hannah with what she was asking for and that was a son. Eli spoke the blessing and God answered. Not for the sake of Hannah or for the sake of Eli, but it was answered for the glory of God.

So the priestly blessing is not dependent upon the one giving the blessing and it is not dependent upon the recipient. The priestly blessing is for the Glory of God. We are to be bestowing blessings upon one another.

The priestly blessing does two things.

1. IT BRINGS GLORY TO GOD

The main goal in the life of a believer is to become Christ-like and bring glory to God. We should continually speak into each other's lives things that would bring glory to God. Being Christ-like brings glory to God. Having God bless you, be gracious to you, and give you peace brings glory to God. Aren't these the things that we desire in our lives and the lives of our children? Yes! So we should be blessing them by saying priestly blessings over them.

We could say over our children, "_____, *may the Lord bless you and keep you and make His face to shine upon you, and be gracious to you and give you peace.*" We could say things that we would like for them to accomplish that would bring God glory.

We could say, "_____, *may God give you a passion for the Lord so that you will love him with all of your heart, mind, soul and strength.*"

"_____, *may the Lord make you into a godly woman who manages her home well and loves her husband deeply.*"

"_____, *may the Lord use you to lead many people into His kingdom.*"

If we notice frustration in our child, perhaps they are impatient. We could ask God to bless them with patience. If we notice our child is lying, we could bless them with truth. We could say, "_____, *may the Lord give you his words and may you not bear false witness here upon the earth.*"

Granted when we are giving blessings, it should not always be to correct a flaw in them. We should also

143

ask God to bless their territory and make them mighty arrows in society to lead the nations.

How many of us have said, "*You are a bad boy*" or "*You will never amount to anything*"? When Jesus came on the scene, he took some fisherman who were still very rough around the edges. He spoke a blessing on them and said in *Matthew 5:13-14 (NIV)* [13] "*You are the salt of the earth. ...* [14] *"You are the light of the world. A city on a hill cannot be hidden.*

These men were not yet salt and one of them never even amounted to being salt or light at all. But Jesus spoke a blessing on them to be all that God intended for them to be.

As parents, during our family altar time, we can place our hands on our children, look them in their eyes, and bless them. Ask the Lord to give you a blessing for each of your children. Do this often and intentionally. Speak blessings on your children, your spouse, and those around you.

Use Scripture to bless your children. Look at the passage in *Ephesians 1:3-4 (NIV)* [3] *Praise be to the God and Father of our Lord Jesus Christ, who has blessed us in the heavenly realms with every spiritual blessing in Christ.* [4] *For he chose us in him before the creation of the world to be holy and blameless in his sight.*

Your blessing could go like this, "_____, *God has blessed you in the heavenly realms with every spiritual blessing in Christ. For he chose you in him before the creation of the world to be holy and blameless in his sight."*

How many kids have grown up and never heard their parents bless them? How many lives could have been directed differently with a spoken blessing over them? What if a parent whose child did not remain pure until marriage would have been given the blessing, *"May the Lord keep you pure until the day of your wedding day and may he bless your union with your spouse."* This would have imparted God's will for the child and given them vision to obey the Lord. It would have also released the priestly blessing. You are the priests and you can declare the priestly blessing for God to bless them.

Genesis 22:17-18 (NIV) *[17]* *I will surely bless you and make your descendants as numerous as the stars in the sky and as the sand on the seashore. Your descendants will take possession of the cities of their enemies,* *[18]* ***and through your offspring all nations on earth will be blessed, because you have obeyed me."***

Many parents may have prayed such things by praying Scriptures over their children, but it is important to speak the blessing verbally over them. Let your children hear the will of God through your words. Let them be encouraged to fulfill all that God has for them. Release the blessings.

Parents can bless them to fulfill specific roles in society: Godly businessmen and women, missionaries, ministers, politicians, or great employees where they work. Husbands can speak blessings over their wives. Wives can speak blessings over their husbands. Children can speak blessings over their parents. Children can speak blessings over their brothers and sisters. Release the priestly blessings in your home!

2. IT BREAKS A CURSE

Another powerful aspect of the priestly blessing is that it can break a curse. Have you ever known someone who was wounded by another through their words and actions? Many times the wounded individual carries this bitterness, anger, and even guilt with them. The Bible says that our words can curse others. *James 3:7-9 (NIV)* [7] *All kinds of animals, birds, reptiles and creatures of the sea are being tamed and have been tamed by man,* [8] *but no man can tame the tongue. It is a restless evil, full of deadly poison.* [9] *With the tongue we praise our Lord and Father, and with it we* **curse men**, *who have been made in God's likeness.*

This curse can be painful. The words and experiences can be imbedded deep within us. How can we be free? First, we must ask God to enable us to forgive them. We must focus our pain on Satan; the one who enabled them to perform such evil actions. Second, we must thank God that we can see the hurtful words and for the ability not to repeat the curse on others. If we have repeated the curse on others, we must ask God to forgive us and ask the person we placed the curse on to forgive us. Third, we must speak a blessing on the offender. It is one thing to say that you have forgiven them, but it is another to speak a blessing on them.

Remember that in *Matthew 12:34 (NIV)* [34] *...For out of the overflow of the heart the mouth speaks.* If you can truly bless the individual from your heart, you will know that you have forgiven them and you are free from the curse. Sometimes the miracle happens while you are giving the blessing. We must teach our children how to bless when they are cursed. We must teach them how to be free when people place an evil curse on them.

1 Peter 3:9 (NIV) [9] *Do not repay evil with evil or insult with insult,* **but with blessing,** *because to this you were called* **so that you may inherit a blessing.** Many times families say evil and hurtful things in their anger. We must ask for forgiveness and learn to say blessings. We must also teach the one who received the curse to say a blessing on the one who offended them. This is not just repeating the words their Mom and Dad tell them to speak, but truly speaking a blessing from their heart out of sincerity and love. Families need to be adding these two powerful elements to their altar times so they can experience the power of God's Word in their lives. Families need to allow the blood of Jesus to cleanse them from all sin and teach them how to walk in love, peace and unity. Christian families are the light of the world and must show people where true freedom is found. It is found in Jesus Christ alone! *John 8:36*

(NIV) [36] So if the Son sets you free, you will be free indeed. John 17:23 (NIV) [23] I in them and you in me. May they be brought to complete unity to let the world know that you sent me and have loved them even as you have loved me.

WORKSHEET FOR FAMILY GOVERNMENT LIFE TRUTH # 6 THE FAMILY IS RESPONSIBLE TO HAVE AN ALTAR

Question: Where should we go when dissension and disunity arise in our family?
Answer: Our responsibility is to come to the altar and heal the issues in our family.

Numbers 6:24-27 (NIV) ²⁴ *"' "The LORD bless you and keep you;* ²⁵ *the LORD make his face shine upon you and be gracious to you;* ²⁶ *the LORD turn his face toward you and give you peace."'* ²⁷ *"So they will put my name on the Israelites, and I will bless them."*

> Write out the Life Truth, question, and answer on one side of an index card and the verse on the other side. Keep it in your Bible for the week. Work on it every day individually and as a family. Have it memorized by next week.

Read Matthew 26:17-18. Where was Jesus going to eat the Passover meal? (House or Church) Many times we have the Lord's Supper (also called communion) at church, but it is okay to have it at home, as a family. The very first Passover meal was done in the homes of the Israelites.

Read 1 Corinthians 11:17-23. Why was Paul upset with them?
Communion means to be in a right relationship with

God. What causes us to <u>not</u> be in a right relationship with God?

Read I John 2:9-11; 3:15. Communion also means to be in a right relationship with one another. If we are not in a right relationship with one another does that affect our relationship with God?

Read I Corinthians 11:23-34. What should we do before we take communion?
What happens if we take communion in an unworthy manner?

Our memory verse is called the priestly blessing. According to Numbers 6:27 who will bless the people for the spoken blessing?
Read I Chronicles 16:2; I Kings 8:55-61
The spoken blessing is a powerful weapon that Jesus has given us. How are we to use it according to this passage? I Peter 3:9

Write out a blessing that you could say to someone from these passages:
Psalm 119:9-16
Ephesians 5:25-33
I Peter 3:1-6
Matthew 28:19-20

Based on this LIFE TRUTH how will you incorporate communion into your family altar times? What commitments will you make to begin speaking priestly blessings over one another?

FAMILY GOVERNMENT
LIFE TRUTH # 7
A FAMILY IS RESPONSIBLE
TO TEACH DISCIPLINE

Discipline molds character and also builds correct behavior. The Biblical word means to instruct, train, and correct. As we learned in the father's responsibilities, we are to bring up our children *"in the training and instruction of the Lord."* As we train, instruct, and correct our children, we are teaching them discipline.

Discipline is learning a way of life. At times, discipline involves punishment for wrong behavior. *Proverbs 13:24 (NIV)* [24] *He who spares the rod hates his son, but he who loves him is careful to discipline him.* We learn two things from this passage; the first is that we hate our son if we do not use discipline to correct his wrong behavior; the second is that to love our children, we are to carefully discipline them.

Discipline is not just an appropriate spanking or correction. It is also the training and the exampling of a righteous life. The word disciple comes from the word discipline. Jesus had twelve disciples with whom He walked and instructed in righteousness. A disciple is one who learns by following another's example. As parents, we should always be the best example in our children's lives.

God commands us to *"go and make disciples of all nations."* We are to go, teach, instruct, and train; being a Christ-likeness to the world. Since a disciple is a follower, and our goal is to be Christ-like, then our example is Jesus. *I John 2:6 (NIV) ⁶ Whoever claims to live in him must walk as Jesus did.* In our Self-Government study, we focused on being transformed into the likeness of Christ: Serving, Praising, Encouraging, Witnessing, Forgiving, Being Holy, and Working.

Our Biblical responsibility, as a family and as a nation, is to raise the righteous. Righteousness is doing what is right and making just judgments. Our God is a righteous God. We must learn His ways and become His followers.

Ezra 9:15 (NIV) ¹⁵ O LORD, God of Israel, you are righteous! As we discipline ourselves and train our children in righteousness, we can experience the promises God has for the righteous.

Proverbs 10:30 (NIV) ³⁰ The righteous will never be uprooted, but the wicked will not remain in the land.

Proverbs 12:3 (NIV) ³ A man cannot be established through wickedness, but the righteous cannot be uprooted.

When a generation turns away from the commands of God, they begin to experience God's discipline. He disciplines us in love to direct us back to His ways.

152

Daniel 9:14 (NIV) ^{14} *The LORD did not hesitate to bring the disaster upon us, for the LORD our God is righteous in everything he does; yet we have not obeyed him.*

God's ways bring blessings and our ways bring trouble. As Christians, we must discipline ourselves to the ways of God so that we can experience His blessings. *Psalm 37:25 (NIV)* ^{25} *I was young and now I am old, yet I have never seen the righteous forsaken or their children begging bread.*

Our generation is not seeing God's protection, provision, or a nation of righteous leaders. The reason is that we are no longer disciplining ourselves to be the righteous.

WHY DOES GOD DISCIPLINE US?

1. Because He loves us.

Proverbs 3:11-12 (NIV) ^{11} *My son, do not despise the LORD's discipline and do not resent his rebuke,* ^{12} *because the LORD disciplines those he loves, as a father the son he delights in.*

Notice this passage in *Hebrews 12:4-10 (NIV)* ^{4} *In your struggle against sin, you have not yet resisted to the point of shedding your blood.* ^{5} *And you have forgotten that word of encouragement that addresses you as sons: "My son, do not make light of the Lord's discipline, and do not lose heart when he rebukes you,* ^{6} *because the Lord disciplines those he loves, and he punishes everyone he*

153

accepts as a son." ⁷ Endure hardship as discipline; God is treating you as sons. For what son is not disciplined by his father? ⁸ If you are not disciplined (and everyone undergoes discipline), then you are illegitimate children and not true sons. ⁹ Moreover, we have all had human fathers who disciplined us and we respected them for it. How much more should we submit to the Father of our spirits and live! ¹⁰ Our fathers disciplined us for a little while as they thought best; but God disciplines us for our good, that we may share in his holiness.

The passage points out that God is a loving father who disciplines us for our own good. It also points out that a loving father will discipline his children. God's discipline is so that we may share in His holiness and be in His presence.

HOW DOES GOD DISCIPLINE US?

1. **Through the weather and natural disasters.** *2 Chronicles 7:13 (NIV) ¹³ "When I shut up the heavens so that there is no rain, or command locusts to devour the land or send a plague among my people,*

2. **Through sicknesses.** *I Corinthians 11:28-30 (NIV) ²⁸ A man ought to examine himself before he eats of the bread and drinks of the cup. ²⁹ For anyone who eats and drinks without recognizing the body of the Lord eats and drinks judgment on*

*himself. [30] That is why many among you are weak
and sick, and a number of you have fallen asleep.*

3. **Through trials.** *James 1:12 (NIV) [12] Blessed is
the man who perseveres under trial, because when
he has stood the test, he will receive the crown of
life that God has promised to those who love him.*

It is through the Lord's discipline that we should be
learning how to trust God more and ultimately
becoming more holy. Hebrews tells us of the
unpleasantness of discipline, as well as the harvest of
righteousness and peace that it produces.

*Hebrews 12:11 (NIV) [11] No discipline seems pleasant at
the time, but painful. Later on, however, it produces a
harvest of righteousness and peace for those who have
been trained by it.*

Discipline from the Lord is not always because we
have done something wrong. However, it is always
used to help us become more holy and to bring God
glory as we become more righteous.

God loves us enough to discipline us and train us in
righteousness. He does it both in love and out of
love. We must have the same attitude as loving
parents when we discipline our children. No
discipline should be done in anger.

HOW DO WE DISCIPLINE OURSELVES TO BE THE RIGHTEOUS?

1. Understand that righteousness comes from God.

Romans 1:17 (NIV) [17] For in the gospel a righteousness from God is revealed, a righteousness that is by faith from first to last, just as it is written: "The righteous will live by faith." I Peter 2:24 (NIV) [24] He himself bore our sins in his body on the tree, so that we might die to sins and live for righteousness; by his wounds you have been healed.

Righteousness comes from God and by faith to those who believe. Righteousness is having the self-control to do what is right. Notice the character that comes in the fruit of the Spirit. *Galatians 5:22-23 (NIV) [22] But the fruit of the Spirit is love, joy, peace, patience, kindness, goodness, faithfulness, [23] gentleness **and self-control**.*

2. We cannot be righteous without being on our knees and asking God for help.

In the last Life Truth, we discussed that families need a family altar. We need to be getting on our knees, asking God to fill us with His Holy Spirit. If we are not praying and asking God for help, then we are trusting in ourselves, forgetting that it is God who makes us righteous. Children need to hear their parents ask God for forgiveness, for help, and for direction.

THE PROCESS OF DISCIPLINE

1. Set Biblical priorities

The Bible and the ministers of God's Word were the main sources of instruction when our nation was founded. Stephen McDowell says in his book, In God We Trust, on page 132, *"Almost everyone owned a Bible and most people could read it. It's ideas shaped their character and thinking more than anything else."*

One of the ways in which the Bible was taught was through catechisms. The catechisms were very similar to the Life Truths that we are memorizing. People would memorize Biblical principles and then discuss how they could apply them to their lives. This whole process took discipline. Memorization is not a strength; it is a discipline and it is hard work. The amount of time taken to memorize scripture can vary with each person but the dedication is always the same.

The Bible speaks often about harvest. Whatever is sown produces a harvest. A seed that is planted eventually produces a plant. Notice this passage in *Hosea 10:12-13 (NIV)* [12] *Sow for yourselves righteousness, reap the fruit of unfailing love, and break up your unplowed ground; for it is time to seek the LORD,* *until he comes and showers righteousness on you. ^{13} But you have planted wickedness, you have reaped evil, you have eaten the fruit of deception. Because you have depended on your own strength and on your many warriors,*

Most Christians would agree that it is very beneficial for their children to memorize verses in the Bible. But many are not disciplining their children to memorize the Bible. Parents are too busy doing other things instead of taking the time necessary to sow the Word into their children. This is a vital step to producing a harvest of righteousness in our nation. How can the Word produce a harvest in our nation if we are not sowing it in our families? This discipline must become one of our main priorities as families.

The opposite of a disciplined person is a sluggard. *Proverbs 20:4 (NIV) ^{4} A sluggard does not plow in season; so at harvest time he looks but finds nothing.* The Bible condemns being slothful and lazy. The fruit of the Spirit gives us self-control, but we have to do our part. *I Corinthians 9:24-27 (NIV) ^{24} Do you not know that in a race all the runners run, but only one gets the prize? Run in such a way as to get the prize. ^{25} Everyone who competes in the games goes into strict training. They do it to get a crown that will not last; but we do it to get a crown that will last forever. ^{26} Therefore I do not run like a man running aimlessly; I do not fight like a man beating the air. ^{27} No, I beat my body and make it my slave so that after I have preached to others, I myself will not be disqualified for the prize.*

We need to be sure that knowledge about God's kingdom and His righteousness is our first priority. *Matthew 6:33 (NIV)* [33] *But seek first his kingdom and his righteousness, and all these things will be given to you as well.* We must make the Bible our main priority by setting spiritual goals for our families. Use the worksheet for this Life Truth to set priorities for your family.

Proverbs 29:17 (NIV) [17] *Discipline your son, and he will give you peace; he will bring delight to your soul.*

2. Remove Temptations

Paul talked about beating his body in order to make it obedient to Christ. He was not referring to a literal beating but a symbolic beating of denying the sinful desires of the flesh. We know about ugly desires like drunkenness, drugs, pornography, adultery, homosexuality, greed, etc... . But do we fight against the "good" things in life that interfere with the time needed for totally seeking God's kingdom? Many times we choose "good" activities that keep us so busy we are unable to sow the Word into our children. We think that we are doing a good job if our children are involved in sports and other extra-curricular activities. But sports and other activities are not helping them memorize the Word which should be the top priority in a Christian family's life.

Jesus said in *Matthew 5:29-30 (NIV)* *[29] If your right eye causes you to sin, gouge it out and throw it away. It is better for you to lose one part of your body than for your whole body to be thrown into hell. [30] And if your right hand causes you to sin, cut it off and throw it away. It is better for you to lose one part of your body than for your whole body to go into hell.*

The sinful desires in our lives that pull us away from pursuing righteousness need to be cut off. If you are an alcoholic, you should not keep alcohol in your refrigerator. If you have a temptation to do drugs, you should not hang out with people who do drugs. If you are too busy to spend time fulfilling your family responsibilities, then something needs to change.

Fathers are to bring their families up in the training and instruction of the Lord. If a father is too busy to read the Word to his family and help them memorize it, then his schedule needs to change. Mothers are to manage the home and help raise the righteous. If a mother has no time to organize chores, plan meals, teach her children the Word, and help raise the righteous, then her schedule needs to change.

3. Make a Plan

Once you have set your Biblical priorities and removed any temptations, it is time to make a plan. Set some goals, make a chart, and allocate specific times to fulfill your priorities. It is very important to

commit your plans to the Lord. *Proverbs 16:3 (NIV)*
3 Commit to the LORD whatever you do, and your plans will succeed. It is important to remember as we make our Biblical plans to discipline ourselves in righteousness that God is in control. We need to always remain open for the Lord's direction as we make our plans. *Proverbs 19:21 (NIV) 21 Many are the plans in a man's heart, but it is the LORD's purpose that prevails.*

Look at what Paul wrote to the Romans. It says in Romans 15:20-25 (NIV) *20 It has always been my ambition to preach the gospel where Christ was not known, so that I would not be building on someone else's foundation. 21 Rather, as it is written: "Those who were not told about him will see, and those who have not heard will understand." 22 This is why I have often been hindered from coming to you. 23 But now that there is no more place for me to work in these regions, and since I have been longing for many years to see you, 24 I plan to do so when I go to Spain. I hope to visit you while passing through and to have you assist me on my journey there, after I have enjoyed your company for a while.*

We see that Paul had a priority to preach the gospel where Christ was not known. Once he had traveled through all the regions, he made plans to go to Spain and stop in Rome. What are your priorities and how will you accomplish them?

4. Maintain order in your home

It is one thing to say you are going to do something and it is another thing to accomplish it. It takes discipline to accomplish tasks. It takes discipline to maintain order in the home. Did you know that depression and stress can be tied to an unorganized life? We get depressed when we do not accomplish certain goals. We get depressed and stressed when our lives are not in order. Children grow and mature best when they have structure and order in their lives.

Some have said, *"Cleanliness is next to Godliness."* While this phrase is not in Scripture, the principles of orderliness are. God is most definitely a God of order. We can look at His creation and understand the significance of His order. In the church, we are also commanded to keep order. *I Corinthians 14:40 (NIV)* [40] *But everything should be done in a fitting and orderly way.*

Men chosen to lead in church must be able to manage their own homes. *I Timothy 3:4-5 (NIV)* [4] *He must manage his own family well and see that his children obey him with proper respect.* [5] *(If anyone does not know how to manage his own family, how can he take care of God's church?)* It would not make sense for the church to be kept in an orderly fashion by leaders whose homes were in disarray. We are to choose our leaders by the way that they keep their homes. Christian adults who keep their families in order are qualified to lead in church and civil government.

Women are to be the managers of their homes. *I Timothy 5:14 (NIV) ···to manage their homes.* A good manager succeeds in their goals. We are to discipline ourselves in fulfilling our God-given responsibilities. An orderly home allows us to accomplish our goals. It helps to relieve stress and depression. It makes the home a place of peace.

Some women might get depressed just hearing such words. They may picture a person with a white glove constantly looking for that little bit of dust. This is not God's intention. It is good to be orderly, keeping our homes neat, but we can also work too hard and never find time to be with the Lord. Keeping the house in order and managing the home has a purpose. The purpose is to have time with the Lord and not be stressed over our ever-present daily responsibilities.

We need time to fulfill our family government responsibilities:

Question: What is God's design for a father?
Answer: God's design for a father is to lead his family, love his wife, and bring his children up in the training and instruction of the Lord.

Question: What is God's design for a mother?
Answer: God's design for a mother is to empower her husband to lead, manage the home, and help raise the righteous.

Question: What is God's design for children?
Answer: God's design for a child is to know Christ, obey authority and grow up to lead in society.

Question: What are we to do with anger?
Answer: Our responsibility is to get rid of man's anger and be kind to one another.

Question: Where should we go when dissension and disunity arise in our family?
Answer: Our responsibility is to come to the altar and heal the issues in our family.

Question: What should we do when our home is getting out of order?
Answer: Our responsibility is discipline ourselves to fulfill God's purposes.

What are the results of maintaining order in the home? Raising up mighty warriors for this generation!

Be honest. Be clean. Be on time. Be respectful. All of these responsibilities are first learned in the home. Children learn responsibilities by fulfilling the goals and tasks that their parents set for them. Parents are to train their children how to be godly citizens. Parents are not to make their children happy all the time. The flesh will never be satisfied. If a parent's goal is to keep their child happy, it is a bottomless pit and a trap.

Children will always say, *"I don't want to."* Or *"I don't like that."* But we are to train them that life is not about their happiness. It is about giving glory to God. How many parents don't want to get up and go to work? How many parents don't want to pay their taxes? How many parents don't want to fix the things that break in their homes? How many parents get tired of changing dirty diapers?

Throughout life, we must to learn to serve God and give Him glory. Our focus is not to be on what we want or desire. A godly worker shows up on time and obeys authority. Children learn to be on time by getting up at a set time. They learn responsibility by fulfilling their chores, doing their homework, memorizing Scriptures, and obeying their parents.

We learn obedience through suffering. This is discipline. It is not pleasant, but it produces a harvest of righteousness. The worker who shows up on time, works hard, and accomplishes more than what was asked of him is promoted by God in society. Look at what the Bible says about how Jesus learned obedience. *Hebrews 5:8 (NIV) [8] Although he was a son, he learned obedience from what he suffered.*

Our responsibility is to raise the righteous. All of us need to learn to do things we do not like to do. Making disciples is also teaching children how to follow our examples. Are we getting up on time? Are we arriving at church on time? Are we having our quiet times, memorizing Scriptures, and obeying

165

authorities? We must set the examples. We must drive the speed limit, pay our bills on time, pay our taxes, and fulfill tasks beyond what is expected of us.

If we give our children a candy bar every time they whine to keep them quiet, what kind of warrior are we raising? If we say, *"Oh, you don't want to memorize. That's OK. Oh, you don't want to read the Bible. That's OK. Oh, you don't want to get up on time. That's OK. Oh, you don't want to do your chores. That's OK."* If your child joined the military to learn discipline, would the officer say, *"What can I do to make you happy?"* Of course not! We shouldn't yell, scream, or belittle our children to get them to obey, but we do need to be consistent.

It is a discipline to be consistent in raising our children. We must combat their whining and help them die to self and live to serve God.

The Bible says in *Psalm 127:4 (NIV)* [4] *Like arrows in the hands of a warrior are sons born in one's youth.* As we teach our children discipline and impress the Word in them, they will grow up to lead our nation in righteousness. Our job as parents is to raise great warriors for the Lord. When we are disloyal, slothful, and undisciplined, it is like having a faulty bow. *Psalm 78:57 (NIV)* [57] *Like their fathers they were disloyal and faithless, as unreliable as a faulty bow.* And in *Hosea 7:16 (NIV)* *16* *They do not turn to the Most High; they are like a faulty bow. Their leaders will fall by the sword because of their insolent words.*

Abraham was a godly man who raised up some mighty arrows. He fulfilled this by bringing his household up in the training and instruction of the Lord. *Genesis 18:18-19 (NIV)* *18* *Abraham will surely become a great and powerful nation, and all nations on earth will be blessed through him.* *19* *For I have chosen him, so that he will direct his children and his household after him to keep the way of the LORD by doing what is right and just, so that the LORD will bring about for Abraham what he has promised him."*

The Bible says in Genesis, Chapter 14, that four kings came together and began to conquer other kingdoms. In verse 8, five kings got together to stop these four kings. The four kings, with all their fighting men, captured the five kingdoms.

The Bible says in *Genesis 14:11-12 (NIV)* *11* *The four kings seized all the goods of Sodom and Gomorrah and all their food; then they went away.* *12* *They also carried off Abram's nephew Lot and his possessions, since he was living in Sodom.*

News of Lot's capture reached Abraham. *Genesis 14:14-16 (NIV)* *14* *When Abram heard that his relative had been taken captive, he called out the 318 trained* men born in his household and went in pursuit as far as *Dan*. So Abraham went to fight the four powerful kingdoms who had been defeating everyone, including the five kingdoms that tried to stand up against them. He did not go with other kingdoms, but with the 318 trained men that were his mighty arrows. Men that Abraham was "*directing his children and his household after him to keep the way of the LORD by doing what is right and just*". Guess which side the Lord was on?

The Bible continues, ^{15} *During the night Abram divided his men to attack them and he routed them, pursuing them as far as Hobah, north of Damascus.* ^{16} *He recovered all the goods and brought back his relative Lot and his possessions, together with the women and the other people.*

With God, no matter how small we may be, we are powerful and mighty. We must begin to discipline ourselves by directing our children to keep the ways of the Lord. For those of you struggling with finances, relationships, and other trials, put God first. Begin memorizing, reading, praying and watching what God will do for you. Seek first His kingdom and His righteousness and He will come through for you!

5. Be people of your word

Making a commitment and keeping your word is very important. As Christians, we have taken on the name of God. We are His children. Our lives are to reflect the character of God. When God speaks, His words will be accomplished. *Isaiah 55:11 (NIV)* [11] *so is my word that goes out from my mouth: It will not return to me empty, but will accomplish what I desire and achieve the purpose for which I sent it.*

We might read this chapter and say,
- *"I'm going to get my life and the life of my family more disciplined."*
- *"We are going to begin reading the word and memorizing more."*
- *"We are going to set our priorities and make a plan."*

It is easy to make commitments. But it is a sin not to keep them. We are to be people of our word. Jesus said it this way in *Matthew 5:37 (NIV)* [37] *Simply let your 'Yes' be 'Yes,' and your 'No,' 'No'; anything beyond this comes from the evil one.* In *James 5:12 (NIV)* [12] *Above all, my brothers, do not swear—not by heaven or by earth or by anything else. Let your "Yes" be yes, and your "No," no, or you will be condemned.*

We need to be people of our word and committed to fulfilling what we say. Are you a person of your word? Do you fulfill what you have said? Never give someone a reason to describe you as complacent. (Complacency: self-satisfaction especially when accompanied by unawareness of actual dangers. Merriam-Webster's 11th Collegiate Dictionary)
Our faulty bows need to be repaired. We need to be aiming our arrows at the enemy who is overtaking

our land. We need to be disciplined in our lives, raising up disciples for Christ who can go out and lead in society as bold, unashamed, prepared warriors for God.

If we don't, the proverbs will be true of this nation. *Proverbs 1:29-33 (NIV)* [29] *Since they hated knowledge and did not choose to fear the LORD,* [30] *since they would not accept my advice and spurned my rebuke,* [31] *they will eat the fruit of their ways and be filled with the fruit of their schemes.* [32] *For the waywardness of the simple will kill them, and the complacency of fools will destroy them;* [33] *but whoever listens to me will live in safety and be at ease, without fear of harm."*

What commitments do you need to make to set Biblical priorities, develop a plan, remove all temptations, raise up mighty warriors, and be people of your word?

WORKSHEET FOR FAMILY GOVERNMENT
LIFE TRUTH #7
THE FAMILY IS RESPONSIBLE
TO TEACH DISCIPLINE

Question: What should we do when our home is getting out of order?
Answer: Our responsibility is to discipline ourselves to fulfill God's purposes.

Hebrews 12:11 (NIV) [11] *No discipline seems pleasant at the time, but painful. Later on, however, it produces a harvest of righteousness and peace for those who have been trained by it.*

> Write out the Life Truth, question, and answer on one side of an index card and the verse on the other side. Keep it in your Bible for the week. Work on it every day individually and as a family. Have it memorized by next week.

According to our memory verse is discipline pleasant?
What are the benefits of discipline?

Read Proverbs 5:21-23. Why will the man die?
Read Proverbs 10:17. What do we do for others when we ignore correction?
Read Proverbs 19:18. What is the warning in this verse?

Discipline is instruction, training, and correction. Our flesh desires to be lazy, but the Spirit is calling us to be disciplined and accomplish the Lord's work here upon the earth.

List by order of importance these responsibilities with 1 being the most important:
- o Be in the Word everyday
- o Be involved in sports or extra-curricular activities
- o Instruct others in the Word
- o Go out to eat
- o Relax and watch TV
- o Go see a movie
- o Pray with your family
- o Memorize Scripture as a family
- o Attend Church
- o Help someone in need
- o Go to work
- o Go on vacation
- o Raise up a Spiritual Leader
- o Raise up a "good" person

Read 1 Cor. 9:24-27. Look at your list. Are the most important responsibilities getting the attention that they deserve? Write down a list of priorities and make a plan to fulfill them. Good intentions are not enough. We need to discipline ourselves to fulfill what is important.

What will need to be removed from your schedule in order to accomplish this?

Based on this LIFE TRUTH how can you encourage your family to accomplish your commitments? Removing "good" things is hard, but the harvest of righteousness is what this generation needs. Pray that God will help you maintain proper order in your home.

FAMILY GOVERNMENT
LIFE TRUTH # 8
THE FAMILY IS RESPONSIBLE
TO TEACH FINANCES

Pastor John Winthrope had a dream when he sent the Pilgrims to America. His "American dream" was for them to arrive and establish a Christian nation. He challenged the group to carefully obey the Word of God so that they would become the "city on a hill" that Jesus spoke about in the Sermon on the Mount. He believed God would bless them if they obeyed God and His commands.

The American dream has changed over the years. It used to mean that a person had the freedom to work hard and build a good life for himself. Individuals had freedom to own property and build their own houses. If you came to America, you had the opportunity to be thrifty, work hard, and establish a home for your family.

In the early years of our nation, individuals paid cash for their homes. Many people even built the homes themselves. They worked hard, saved their money, and built their homes as God blessed them with the necessary resources. Today, the American dream has turned from a "hard work ethic" to a "get rich quick" belief. We want what we want and we want it now. We have fallen into the "status trap" of success.

Owning a certain type of home, car, and clothes now means that we have achieved the American dream. We see this "love for money and things" in the popularity of many TV game shows. The show, "Who Wants to be a Millionaire?" has 240,000 people calling in to be contestants on specific entry days. The popularity of this show, and others like it, illustrates our nation's desire to be rich. We also see greed in our nation as lotteries continue to grow and people continue to go deeper and deeper in debt. What is God's plan for our nation and it's finances? Is it to acquire more things? Is it to just make people more comfortable and happy while they're here on this earth? The Bible says in *Ecclesiastes 5:15 (NIV)* [15] *Naked a man comes from his mother's womb, and as he comes, so he departs. He takes nothing from his labor that he can carry in his hand.* This is a sobering verse against the goal of our current American dream. We come into the world with nothing and we leave this world with nothing. We must never forget that we will be judged by how we handled what God provided for us.

The Bible also says in *Psalm 24:1 (NIV)* [1] *The earth is the LORD's, and everything in it, the world, and all who live in it.* This verse reminds us that God owns everything. He is the creator of it all. If we take credit for anything that we acquire, then we are mistaken. We must realize that all of our resources come from the Lord.

If God is the owner of it all, then we are His stewards. A steward utilizes and manages another's resources. Scripturally, we are to manage whatever God gives us for His glory and His divine purpose. Is the current American dream fulfilling God's purpose?

Today, much of the Church has fallen prey to the current lie of the American dream. We have taken our eyes off Scripture and the many ways God has commanded us to handle finances. This is one more area that is out of order in our nation. As Christian families, we must return to God's Word for instruction and then train our nation by our example. This area of discipline will take self-control, repentance, and a new mindset.

The more I study these God-ordained institutions, the more I realize that I need to get things in order in my own life. Finances is an area where I need to repent and learn better how to apply God's principles. Many Christians might disagree with me since I have a good credit score and a nice house for my family. If the only thing that God wanted me to do with my finances was to provide for my family and build a nice house, then I would be doing well. But God desires more of me than just acquiring things to bless myself and my family while I'm here on this earth.

The Bible has a lot to say in the area of finances. There are over 2000 Scriptures that deal with money. We won't be able to cover all 2000 in this chapter, but we will look at some specific Biblical guidelines that apply to us all.

Currently, our nation has a tremendous national debt. We get upset at our government for their lack of responsibility in handling money, but we must remember that building blocks for a Godly nation begin in the home. The national debt is bad, but look at the debt of the American family across our country. Are families handling their money in a Christ-like manner? When individuals, families, and churches get their finances in order, our government's finances will finally begin to get in order.

Biblical Principles in the area of finances:

1. Keep a Heavenly focus.

We can get so consumed with the here and now that we forget about the Day of Judgment. *1 Timothy 6:7 (NIV) 7 For we brought nothing into the world, and we can take nothing out of it.* There is life after death. We are going to be spending an eternity in either heaven or hell. We have the opportunity right now to choose to be in heaven with Jesus. The way we manage things on this earth is a sign of who we are obeying. We must commit to make Jesus our Lord in all areas of our lives.

Look at what Jesus said in *Luke 6:10-12 (NIV) 10 "Whoever can be trusted with very little can also be* *trusted with much, and whoever is dishonest with very little will also be dishonest with much. ¹¹ So if you have not been trustworthy in handling worldly wealth, who will trust you with true riches? ¹² And if you have not been trustworthy with someone else's property, who will give you property of your own?* How we handle our worldly wealth is a test.

We need to keep our focus on true riches, not the world's wealth that people seem to desperately chase after. Look at what else Jesus said in *Luke 19:15-19 (NIV) ¹⁵ "He was made king, however, and returned home. Then he sent for the servants to whom he had given the money, in order to find out what they had gained with it. ¹⁶ "The first one came and said, 'Sir, your mina has earned ten more.' ¹⁷ "'Well done, my good servant!' his master replied. 'Because you have been trustworthy in a very small matter, take charge of ten cities.' ¹⁸ "The second came and said, 'Sir, your mina has earned five more.' ¹⁹ "His master answered, 'You take charge of five cities.'*

These servants managed their money well. As a result, their master not only blessed them because they were trustworthy with their wealth, but also increased their responsibilities. One was given charge over ten cities and another over five cities. Jesus explained that it was because they had been trustworthy in a very small matter. Jesus was referring to the handling of money upon this earth. We can get so consumed with money here on earth that it becomes a huge issue for us. The truth is that

178

God sees our handling of money as a very small matter compared to our responsibilities in heaven.

2. Be content with what you have

This is not the current advertising slogan in America. Everywhere we turn, someone is trying to tell us that we need more, we need better, and we need newer. Paul wrote this in *Philippians 4:12 (NIV)* [12] *I know what it is to be in need, and I know what it is to have plenty. I have learned the secret of being content in any and every situation, whether well fed or hungry, whether living in plenty or in want.* Paul calls this wisdom of contentment a secret. To be content means to be at peace with what God provides for you. Paul said that he was content being in need, but had also learned the secret of being content in any and every situation. When we see something that we want, are we content? When we want the new iPhone or the newest car, are we content? Unfortunately, in America it is so easy to get what we want when we want it. If we want the new phone or the new car, we can just get a loan and buy it. Is this how God intends for us to live? Should we just buy what we want?

I'm not saying that it is wrong to have an iPhone or a new car; but I am saying that we need to learn to be content with what we have. Can you be content without the new iPhone or the new car? Being content is knowing that these materialistic things do not matter in light of eternity. Our flesh can consume us with what we want. The *"we need a new nature"* Life Truth reminds us that our flesh cannot be satisfied. If we open ourselves up to the *"we must have the latest and greatest"* it eventually consumes our minds. Every time a new product is advertised, we are tempted just as an alcoholic desires a drink. How does an alcoholic learn to stop drinking? One day at a time by fasting from the desire. How does a materialistic person deny themself from the fleshly things that they crave? Be in prayer; renew your mind, and fast from looking up information on what you want. Don't consume yourself with what you want. Consume yourself with God's Word and by getting to know Him. Ask the Lord what His will is for your life.

 I'm not saying that having an iPhone is sinful. But I am saying that if you cannot be content without one you have a problem. Our relationship with Jesus should be the only thing that fills us. Materialistic things in this world only bring us discontentment. Eventually they all wear out or let us down. Look at what it says in *Hebrews 13:5-6 (NIV)* *⁵ Keep your lives free from the love of money and be content with what you have, because God has said, "Never will I leave you; never will I forsake you." ⁶ So we say with confidence, "The Lord is my helper; I will not be afraid. What can man do to me?"*

When we are free from our sinful desires, we are content. Content people sleep well and have a joy about them. Discontent people worry about bills and how they can buy more things. Focusing on pleasing ourselves is not the life that God wants His people to lead. There are no apps that get people into heaven! We are only free when we love God more than any materialistic thing.

Realize the dangers of debt

Some teach that a person should never get into debt. Some teach that it is okay to have debt as long as you can make your payments. Debt is owing something to someone else. The Bible warns against being in debt to another. *Proverbs 22:7 (NIV)* [7] *The rich rule over the poor, and the borrower is servant to the lender.* One of the powers of the antichrist is that he will enslave the world by controlling the ability to buy and sell. Christ wants us to be free. This includes wanting us to be free financially as well.

Debt can be an ugly monster that entraps us and enslaves us for many years. A person who borrows money is enslaving themselves to the lender by making a commitment to pay the debt back with interest. High interest can cause a person to pay three or even four times what the item is really worth. Late payments cause people to get even higher interest rates or penalties that can enslave people even more.

Does God really want us to pay three or four times what things are really worth? Is this a good financial decision? Some use the verse in the King James version of the Bible that implies all debt is sinful. *Romans 13:8 (KJV)* *8 Owe no man any thing, but to love one another: for he that loveth another hath fulfilled the law.* The NIV translates the verse like this in *Romans 13:8 (NIV)* *8 Let no debt remain outstanding, except the continuing debt to love one another, for he who loves his fellowman has fulfilled the law.* I think the NIV translation is a better one in light of the context of the verse. The prior passage is talking about paying what you owe. *Romans 13:6-7 (NIV)* *6 This is also why you pay taxes, for the authorities are God's servants, who give their full time to governing. 7 Give everyone what you owe him: If you owe taxes, pay taxes; if revenue, then revenue; if respect, then respect; if honor, then honor.*

The Bible teaches that it is good to loan someone money. *Leviticus 25:35-38 (NIV)* *35 "'If one of your countrymen becomes poor and is unable to support himself among you, help him as you would an alien or a temporary resident, so he can continue to live among you. 36 Do not take interest of any kind from him, but fear your God, so that your countryman may continue to live among you. 37 You must not lend him money at interest or sell him food at a profit. 38 I am the LORD your God, who brought you out of Egypt to give you the land of Canaan and to be your God.* You'll notice that God commanded the Israelites to help the person in need without even charging interest.

Although pawn shops did not exist, they did hold things in pledge for any money that was loaned out. *Deuteronomy 24:10-13 (NIV)* *10 When you make a loan* *of any kind to your neighbor, do not go into his house to get what he is offering as a pledge. ^{11} Stay outside and let the man to whom you are making the loan bring the pledge out to you. ^{12} If the man is poor, do not go to sleep with his pledge in your possession. ^{13} Return his cloak to him by sunset so that he may sleep in it. Then he will thank you, and it will be regarded as a righteous act in the sight of the LORD your God.*

You will notice that God allowed provision for a person to get a loan and for a person to loan money. The focus is on the generosity of the lender by helping someone in need. Too often, in our generation, we are taking loans out for what we want instead of taking loans out for what we need.

When we take out a loan, it is vital to have the ability to pay it back. *Psalm 37:21 (NIV) ^{21} The wicked borrow and do not repay, but the righteous give generously;* It is also important to seek Godly council from the Word on such decisions. Questions need to be asked before enslavement is upon us. Is this something that I need or is this something that I want? Does God want me to have this? Is this something that I will be able to use for God's glory and for His purpose?

Our generation is taking on way too much debt. We are not fulfilling God's purpose in our lives with our money. Many people in America are doing what Jesus condemns in Scripture. Jesus tells a parable about a selfish greedy man. *Luke 12:18-21 (NIV) ^{18} "Then he said, 'This is what I'll do. I will tear down my barns and* *build bigger ones, and there I will store all my grain and my goods. [19] And I'll say to myself, "You have plenty of good things laid up for many years. Take life easy; eat, drink and be merry."' [20] "But God said to him, 'You fool! This very night your life will be demanded from you. Then who will get what you have prepared for yourself?' [21] "This is how it will be with anyone who stores up things for himself but is not rich toward God."*

God's design for money is not that we would store it up for ourselves; but that in our excess, we would help others in need. When Judgment Day comes, what do we want God to say about how we handled what He blessed us with? Did we store it up for ourselves so that we could take life easy or did we meet people's needs and help them see the love of God? Many people can't help someone in need because they are already so enslaved in debt that they can barely get by. Many people buy a house, then sell that house and buy a bigger and better house. They may even do this several times throughout their lifetime. Not only do they end up with really big houses, but they buy two or three cars and lots of things to put in their houses. They use credit cards to acquire these things which means that they are paying more for the items than they are worth. Many Christians today, not only mishandle their finances in this way, but they neglect to give God the 10 percent that He requires of them. Debt can have many sinful symptoms. You may take out a loan because you are impatient. You may take out a loan because of pride. You may take out a loan because you think you deserve a new car or name brand clothes. You may take out a loan because you're too lazy to earn the bread you eat. You may take out a loan because of fear or unbelief that God will provide for all your needs.

What if God said, *"I have to go away, but I need you to buy me a house. Here is some money. I will be back in a few weeks."* When He returns what would you show him? Would you say, *"Well Lord, I put your money down on a really big house. The payments are very affordable over the next 30 years."* What if He asks you how much He will end up paying for that big house? Would you be comfortable telling Him that He will pay four times what the home is worth? Would that be a good deal? Would that be a wise financial decision?

In most cases, mortgage payments eat up a family's income every month. For other families, it's the mortgage, car, and credit card payments that consume the budget. Are we being good stewards when we overpay for things? Is this what God wants? No! God wants us to be content with what we have. He wants us to live within our means. He wants us to wait upon Him and trust Him for His provisions.

The Bible is clear that we are not to cosign on a loan for someone else either. *Proverbs 22:26-27 (NIV)* *26 Do not be a man who strikes hands in pledge or puts up security for debts; 27 if you lack the means to pay,* your very bed will be snatched from under you. This is enslavement that we are to avoid.

3. Realize the types of poverty

Poverty can be from laziness. *Proverbs 6:6-11 (NIV) 6 Go to the ant, you sluggard; consider its ways and be wise! 7 It has no commander, no overseer or ruler, 8 yet it stores its provisions in summer and gathers its food at harvest. 9 How long will you lie there, you sluggard? When will you get up from your sleep? 10 A little sleep, a little slumber, a little folding of the hands to rest– 11 and poverty will come on you like a bandit and scarcity like an armed man.*

You see the process of storing one's wealth here, in order to have provisions in the future. This is a Biblical teaching and Christians should heed this advice. We should be storing up for the future. Are you storing up? Are your debts so high that there is no room to store up? Are you paying three times what things are worth, therefore making it a long time before you can store anything up? Many of the things people are overpaying for are depreciating as soon as they buy them.

The Bible says that hard work brings a man wealth. *Proverbs 10:4 (NIV) 4 Lazy hands make a man poor, but diligent hands bring wealth.* Diligent hands bring wealth not debt.

Poverty can be from God's discipline. In the book of Malachi, it talks about the nation that is robbing God in their offerings. The consequence to robbing God is a curse from God. *Malachi 3:8-9 (NIV)* *8 "Will a man rob God? Yet you rob me. "But you ask, 'How do we rob you?' "In tithes and offerings. 9 You are under a curse–the whole nation of you–because you are robbing me.* The whole nation was under a curse because of their disobedience in bringing in the tithes. Many Christians in our nation do not bring in their tithes and offerings. We are under a curse because of it.

Proverbs 6:23-26 (NIV) 23 For these commands are a lamp, this teaching is a light, and the corrections of discipline are the way to life, 24 keeping you from the immoral woman, from the smooth tongue of the wayward wife. 25 Do not lust in your heart after her beauty or let her captivate you with her eyes, 26 for the prostitute reduces you to a loaf of bread, and the adulteress preys upon your very life. If you allow yourself to get into an immorality like adultery, drunkenness, greed, etc… there is a good chance that God will discipline you with poverty.

Poverty can be a test. God tested Job and he placed him in poverty. This was Job's response to the test of poverty. *Job 1:20-21 (NIV) 20 At this, Job got up and tore his robe and shaved his head. Then he fell to the ground in worship 21 and said: "Naked I came from my mother's womb, and naked I will depart. The LORD gave and the LORD has taken away; may the name of the*

LORD be praised." Would you praise God if you lost it all? Are you trusting your finances for your security or are you trusting the Lord for your security?

4. **Realize God's design for a nation**

Debt is bondage. It is not God's intention for a nation. When a nation turns away from the commands of God, one of the curses that God allows is debt. Another will rise up among us and enslave us in bondage. *Deuteronomy 28:43-44 (NIV)* *43 The alien who lives among you will rise above you higher and higher, but you will sink lower and lower. 44 He will lend to you, but you will not lend to him. He will be the head, but you will be the tail.*

God's desire for a nation is for them to bless others and show them His provisions. *Deuteronomy 28:12 (NIV) 12 The LORD will open the heavens, the storehouse of his bounty, to send rain on your land in season and to bless all the work of your hands. You will lend to many nations but will borrow from none.* The ability to bless others is dependent upon our obedience to Him and His commands. The storehouse is not for us to build bigger barns for selfish reasons but to bless others. *Genesis 18:18 (NIV) 18 Abraham will surely become a great and powerful nation, and all nations on earth will be blessed through him.*

We are to be the lenders and not the borrowers. We are not to be just any lenders; we are to be very gracious in our dealings just as God is gracious to us.

Ezekiel 18:5-9 (NIV) [5] *"Suppose there is a righteous man who does what is just and right. ...*[7] *He does not oppress anyone, but returns what he took in pledge for a loan. He does not commit robbery but gives his food to the hungry and provides clothing for the naked.* [8] *He does not lend at usury or take excessive interest. He withholds his hand from doing wrong and judges fairly between man and man.* [9] *He follows my decrees and faithfully keeps my laws. That man is righteous; he will surely live, declares the Sovereign LORD.*

We are commanded to be openhanded to all, but we are also told to treat fellow believers with extra care. *Deuteronomy 15:11 (NIV)* [11] *There will always be poor people in the land. Therefore I command you to be openhanded toward your brothers and toward the poor and needy in your land.* **We cannot be openhanded when we are in bondage to our debts.**

Deuteronomy 15:12-15 (NIV) [12] *If a fellow Hebrew, a man or a woman, sells himself to you and serves you six years, in the seventh year you must let him go free.* [13] *And when you release him, do not send him away empty-handed.* [14] *Supply him liberally from your flock, your threshing floor and your winepress. Give to him as the LORD your God has blessed you.* [15] *Remember that you were slaves in Egypt and the LORD your God redeemed you. That is why I give you this command today.*

The Israelites were allowed to charge interest to foreigners, but not to fellow believers. *Deuteronomy*

23:20 (NIV) [20] You may charge a foreigner interest, but not a brother Israelite, so that the LORD your God may bless you in everything you put your hand to in the land you are entering to possess. The interest could not be excessive. It had to be fair. *Proverbs 28:8 (NIV) [8] He who increases his wealth by exorbitant interest amasses it for another, who will be kind to the poor.*

Even though loaning money and acquiring debt was part of the nation of Israel, their primary goal was to be debt free and to be able to help others. God wants us to be free from enslavement and able to minister to others. While getting a loan and going into debt is a negative, God seems to allow it for some purchases. However, we should always be doing what we can to get out of debt.

Deuteronomy 15:1-6 (NIV) [1] At the end of every seven years you must cancel debts. [2] This is how it is to be done: Every creditor shall cancel the loan he has made to his fellow Israelite. He shall not require payment from is fellow Israelite or brother, because the LORD's time for canceling debts has been proclaimed. [3] You may require payment from a foreigner, but you must cancel any debt your brother owes you. [4] However, there should be no poor among you, for in the land the LORD your God is giving you to possess as your inheritance, he will richly bless you, [5] if only you fully obey the LORD your God and are careful to follow all these commands I am giving you today. [6] For the LORD your God will bless you as he has promised, and you will lend to many nations but will borrow from none. You will rule over many nations but none will rule over you.

When we get off of the Biblical focus of helping others with our excess, then the curses begin to fall. We must repent and learn how to live within our means. We must repent and learn how to save before we purchase items. We must repent of the excessive interests that we are paying. We must repent of the bad stewardship examples that we are setting.

What Financial Principles should we be living by?

1. God is our provider and He promises to meet our daily needs.

God desires to bless us. He promises to meet our needs. We get confused with our needs and our wants. We must learn how to be content with what God gives us and stop trying to build our own kingdom here upon the earth. *I Timothy 6:6-8 (NIV)* *6 But godliness with contentment is great gain. 7 For we brought nothing into the world, and we can take nothing out of it. 8 But if we have food and clothing, we will be content with that.* Notice that there is not even a home listed here. Paul says, *"that if we have food and clothing, we will be content with that."* Are we manipulating things to get what we want instead of waiting on the Lord?

2. God desires that we ask Him and thank Him for our provisions.

The Bible says that, "*we have not because we ask not.*" God longs to provide for us, but He wants us to ask Him. He wants us to realize that He owns it all and that He can take care of us. Jesus taught us to pray in *Luke 11:3 (NIV)* [3] *Give us each day our daily bread.*

God desires for us to ask Him for even the basic things. *1 Thessalonians 5:18 (NIV)* [18] *give thanks in all circumstances, for this is God's will for you in Christ Jesus.* Whatever the Lord blesses us with, we are to be thankful. We are not to be looking at all the ads and our next door neighbor's things. That is coveting. We are to be asking God to provide for us. We are to be making sure that everything we have is being used for His glory and for His purpose.

3. Seek Godly counsel before making a big purchase.

When we get the desire to make a purchase, we need to be asking ourselves some questions. Would God want me to have this? Is this something that I can use for God's glory and to further His kingdom? Whenever we are about to make a big purchase, especially if it involves debt, we should be asking others if they think it is a wise decision. *Proverbs 15:22 (NIV)* [22] *Plans fail for lack of counsel, but with many advisers they succeed.* We need to find someone who understands the enslavement of debt, and is committed to being free, and ask them if our decision is wise. There are many Christians today who would say, *"If you can afford the payments, go for it."* But affording the monthly payments should not be our only determining factor.

4. Do all you can to get out of and stay out of debt.

Discipline yourselves by doing all you can to get out and stay out of debt. Debt is enslavement and it causes us to miss opportunities to help others. *Proverbs 22:7 (NIV) ⁷ The rich rule over the poor, and the borrower is servant to the lender.* The result of a godly nation is that the people become debt free and lend help to others. The curse of a nation is that another rises up among us and enslaves us in debt. We must begin to do all we can to get out of debt by making wise decisions.

5. Use our excess in provisions to minister to others.

God desires to bless you with more than you need in order to bless another. The Bible says that our plenty is to supply what others need. Many times our plenty is not used to help others. Unfortunately, it is used to buy bigger and better things for ourselves. We should not be so attached to the things on this earth that we would not sell them to help another. Jesus said this in *Luke 12:33 (NIV) ³³ Sell your possessions and give to the poor. Provide purses for yourselves that will not wear out, a treasure in heaven that will not be exhausted, where no thief comes near and no moth destroys.*

Look at the example for the church of Acts. *Acts 4:34-35 (NIV) [34] There were no needy persons among them. For from time to time those who owned lands or houses sold them, brought the money from the sales [35] and put it at the apostles' feet, and it was distributed to anyone as he had need.*

The Bible is clear that if we have debts, we are to pay them and pay them on time. It would not be right to help someone in need and neglect the commitments of our own debt. This is why it is important to do all we can to get rid of and stay out of debt. We can help more people; storing up for ourselves treasures in heaven. We are to be using our excess to minister to others and to take care of our families. When the church of Acts was selling land and houses, they most likely owned them and did not have debt. Their excess enabled them to give to those in need.

6. Learn to be patient and wait upon the Lord.

Patience is not a current American virtue. We are spoiled and lazy and do not want to wait for what we have. This is sin. *James 5:11 (NIV) [11] As you know, we consider blessed those who have persevered. You have heard of Job's perseverance and have seen what the Lord finally brought about. The Lord is full of compassion and* mercy. When Job lost it all, he did not go to the bank to start over. He persevered, trusted in God, and waited for God to provide for Him. After Job's perseverance through the trial, God doubled what He had lost. We need to learn how to persevere, work hard, save, pray, and wait on the Lord. Just because we want it, doesn't mean that we should have it now. We must make sure that it is something that God desires for us to have. Lack of provision could be God saying "No" to whatever it is you are wanting. When God provides the funds for you to purchase it, that could be the "Yes" you are looking for.

Satan loves the trap of easy credit and easy loans. He loves to enslave us in any way that He can. We must be patient with the Lord, keep His ways, and wait for Him to bless us. We must keep obeying all of God's commands and build a relationship with Him and His Word. We must bring in our tithes and thank Him for what He has provided us with. Persevere and wait for God. *Proverbs 3:9 (NIV)* *⁹ Honor the LORD with your wealth, with the first fruits of all your crops;*

Notice this passage in Psalms. *Psalm 37:34 (NIV)* *³⁴ Wait for the LORD and keep his way. He will exalt you to inherit the land; when the wicked are cut off, you will see it.* Don't be envious of others who have not waited on God. Most of them are deep in debt and have many issues. **Allow God to gradually provide for you and do all you can to get out of and stay out of debt.**

195

7. Excel in the grace of giving.

Avoid the "take life easy" mindset and look for people to minister to. Keep your Judgment Day in focus and remember that it is the Kingdom of Heaven we are living for. Many times we get focused upon the here and now and we begin to build our kingdom here.

If you went to a funeral and you learned that the man being honored lived his life to help others, you would say, *"What an honorable man."* What if you learned that the man could have purchased a big fancy home, but instead he bought a moderate home and helped poorer families in need? This man, even if he was not a Christian, would be honored as a good man. This is the kind of life that God intended for His children to live upon the earth. It is one example of why God says, *"Well done my good and faithful servant."*

2 Corinthians 8:1-15 (NIV) [1] *And now, brothers, we want you to know about the grace that God has given the Macedonian churches.* [2] *Out of the most severe trial, their overflowing joy and their extreme poverty welled up in rich generosity.* [3] *For I testify that they gave as much as they were able, and even beyond their ability. Entirely on their own.* To give beyond one's ability means that they sacrificed and went without. They gave up what they needed for a while in order for another to be blessed.

196

The passage continues *⁴ they urgently pleaded with us for the privilege of sharing in this service to the saints. ⁵ And they did not do as we expected, but they gave themselves first to the Lord and then to us in keeping with God's will.* Good works cannot save anyone. We must give ourselves first to the Lord for our salvation and then allow Him to love others through us. This is in keeping with God's will.

*⁶ So we urged Titus, since he had earlier made a beginning, to bring also to completion this act of grace on your part. ⁷ **But just as you excel in everything--in faith, in speech, in knowledge, in complete earnestness and in your love for us--see that you also <u>excel in this grace of giving</u>.** ⁸ I am not commanding you, but I want to test the sincerity of your love by comparing it with the earnestness of others. ⁹ **For you know the grace of our Lord Jesus Christ, that though he was rich, yet for your sakes he became poor, so that you through his poverty might become rich.***

Jesus is who we are to follow and it is His character that we are to display to the world. Jesus sacrificed so that others could be blessed. We are to excel in this grace of giving. In doing so, we will be storing for ourselves treasures in heaven. We need to sacrifice so that others can have. This is excelling in the grace of giving. It is also obeying what Jesus said, *"Sell your possessions and give to the poor."*

10 And here is my advice about what is best for you in this matter: Last year you were the first not only to give but also to have the desire to do so. 11 Now finish the work, so that your eager willingness to do it may be matched by your completion of it, according to your means. 12 For if the willingness is there, the gift is acceptable according to what one has, not according to what he does not have.

We can begin this grace giving no matter how little we can give. Even if we have accumulated a lot of debt, we can still give our ten percent to God and other offerings to help those in need. God will bless you more and more, as you begin to grow in this grace of giving.

Look at what Paul says in the next chapter about God blessing us for giving to others. **2** *Corinthians 9:6-11 (NIV) 6 Remember this: Whoever sows sparingly will also reap sparingly, and whoever sows generously will also reap generously. 7 Each man should give what he has decided in his heart to give, not reluctantly or under compulsion, for God loves a cheerful giver. 8 And God is able to make all grace abound to you, so that in all things at all times, having all that you need, you will abound in every good work. 9 As it is written: "He has scattered abroad his gifts to the poor; his righteousness endures forever." 10 Now he who supplies seed to the sower and bread for food will also supply and increase your store of seed and will enlarge the harvest of your righteousness. 11 You will be made rich in every way so that you can be generous on every occasion, and through us your generosity will result in thanksgiving to God.*

Paul concludes this thought of excelling in our grace giving by reminding people that our excess is to help others and not to build bigger barns. *¹³ Our desire is not that others might be relieved while you are hard pressed, but that there might be equality. ¹⁴ **At the present time your plenty will supply what they need, so that in turn their plenty will supply what you need.** Then there will be equality, ¹⁵ as it is written: "He who gathered much did not have too much, and he who gathered little did not have too little."*

WORKSHEET FOR FAMILY GOVERNMENT
LIFE TRUTH # 8
THE FAMILY IS RESPONSIBLE
TO TEACH FINANCES

Question: How should Christians view debt?
Answer: Christians should do all they can to get out of and stay out of debt.

Proverbs 22:7 (NIV) [7] *The rich rule over the poor, and the borrower is servant to the lender.*

> Write out the Life Truth, question, and answer on one side of an index card and the verse on the other side. Keep it in your Bible for the week. Work on it every day individually and as a family. Have it memorized by next week.

Circle the Biblical purposes for money:

- o To buy whatever I want
- o To provide for our needs
- o To share with those in need
- o For our security
- o To measure my success by
- o To confirm direction in my life

Read Proverbs 23:4. What is the main point of the verse?
How do some people wear themselves out to get rich?

Read Proverbs 6:6-11. The ant S_____ to have provisions for later. The Sluggard is lazy and what will his end be?

Read Ecclesiastes 5:10. Is it a good decision to borrow money and pay three to four times what something is worth?   What would be a better plan? (Remember the ant?)

Read Matthew 13:22. Debt can be one way that chokes our fruitfulness. What kinds of things could deceive us into getting in too much debt?

Read 1 Timothy 6:9-10. What is the a root of all kinds of evil? L_____ of M_____

Read 2 Corinthians 8:7-15; 9:6-11. What is the good works that the Scripture is referring to?

Read Psalm 15:1-5. Usury is interest. The righteous man lends his money without usury. If we are trapped in debt and unable to have a savings account how can we lend or give to others? We can't. God's design for His people is for them to be the lenders and not the borrowers. Read Deut. 15:6-8.

Read Luke 12:13-34. V15. A man's life does not consist in what?
V33. What are we to do to gain treasures in heaven?

Based on this LIFE TRUTH, how can you encourage your family to stay out of debt? If your family is in debt, what will be your plan to getting out of debt?

FAMILY GOVERNMENT
LIFE TRUTH # 9
THE FAMILY IS RESPONSIBLE
TO PRACTICE HOSPITALITY

Light is the source that produces illumination. A candle has fire, a lamp has a bulb, and the earth has the sun. Jesus called us to be the light of the world. As humans, we are full of darkness and are unable to produce a "spiritual" light. When we become Christians, we are filled with Jesus, the "light" of the world. *John 8:12 (NIV)[12] When Jesus spoke again to the people, he said, "I am the light of the world. Whoever follows me will never walk in darkness, but will have the light of life."*

In the Scriptures, light is symbolic for goodness and obedience to God's commands. Jesus exemplified this as He displayed compassion, love, mercy, and gentleness. We are able to increase the brightness and effectiveness of our "light" when we spend time with Jesus and His Word. The light in us should reflect a godly character that's easily recognizable to others as one belonging to Jesus.

In the Old Testament, Moses went up on the mountain and received the Ten Commandments. When he returned, his face was glowing. *Exodus 34:29-30 (NIV) [29] When Moses came down from Mount Sinai with the two tablets of the Testimony in his hands, he was not aware that his face was radiant because he* *had spoken with the LORD. ³⁰ When Aaron and all the Israelites saw Moses, his face was radiant, and they were afraid to come near him.* The Scriptures say that his face was radiant because he had spoken with the Lord. Moses's face glowed so much that he had to put on a veil. Gradually, Moses's face lost it's glow and he was able to remove the veil.

Paul spoke about this incident in his letter to the Corinthians. *2 Corinthians 3:17-18 (NIV) ¹⁷ Now the Lord is the Spirit, and where the Spirit of the Lord is, there is freedom. ¹⁸ And we, who with unveiled faces all reflect the Lord's glory, are being transformed into his likeness with ever-increasing glory, which comes from the Lord, who is the Spirit.*

Paul is telling the Christians that the Spirit of the Lord dwells in them because of Christ's death and resurrection. In the Old Testament, the Spirit's presence was powerful but then it would fade away. However, in the New Testament, God's radiant Spirit only increases. Paul says that the Lord's glory is ever-increasing in our lives. God's plan is that we continually transform into the likeness of Christ! *Romans 5:5 (NIV) ⁵ And hope does not disappoint us, because God has poured out his love into our hearts by the Holy Spirit, whom he has given us.* God's love being poured into our hearts makes our light brighter and brighter. As we work on ourselves in self-government our light increases. By committing to serve, praise, encourage, witness, forgive, work, and be holy; our godly characteristics increase and we are able to shine brighter for God's glory.

Our light is also to be seen in our homes. The Biblical roles and responsibilities of family members in the home should be an example for others. Our homes are to become ministry centers to show the world the gospel of Christ. This Biblical discipline is called hospitality. The word hospitality comes from the word hospital. The word hospital means a place where we care for the needs of others. Peter reminds us of the role we have in using our homes as ministry centers in *I Peter 4:9 (NIV) ⁹ Offer hospitality to one another without grumbling.* We need to pass on to others the truth about Jesus and His Word, so they can experience the true freedom, peace, and joy that only He gives. This message needs to be shared in our homes.

Peter tells us that we are to offer hospitality without grumbling. To grumble is to be unhappy or discontent with the responsibility you are given. When the Scriptures tell us to offer hospitality to one another, it commands us to do it with a cheerful spirit; or a willing spirit that desires to minister to others.

The only people who would not be expected to offer their homes as ministry centers would be people who do not have a home. If you are a Christian, and you have a home, then you are to use it to minister to others.

Here are some common excuses that people use to get out of this responsibility:

- o My home is not big enough.
- o My home is way too cluttered.
- o I would be embarrassed to have anyone over.
- o I do not have anything to offer them.
- o I am not qualified to minister to anyone.

In spite of the excuses that people use to get out of the responsibility of being hospitable towards others, the command is still there. There are no clauses in Scripture to let us off the hook. If we are born again, then we have the ability to minister to others. Our homes may not be the biggest or the grandest, but they are what the Lord has provided for us. They are to be used for His kingdom and His glory. Hospitality is a powerful ministry and we need to understand its importance.

Often the early church did not have buildings where they could meet. As people were born again, they needed places to gather and hold their corporate worship services. The Scriptures reveal how hospitality was used for these church services: *Romans 16:5 (NIV) ⁵ Greet also the church that **meets at their house**. 1 Corinthians 16:19 (NIV) ¹⁹ The churches in the province of Asia send you greetings. Aquila and Priscilla greet you warmly in the Lord, and so does the church that **meets at their house**.*

Homes are to be ministry centers. The Christian home is many things. It is a place for the family to come together and worship God at the family altar. It is a place to train and instruct children in the ways of God. It is a place to minister to those in need of a bed, a meal, or a listening ear. It is a place to invite people to come and witness what you are learning in the Lord.

Conflict, discontentment, strife, bitterness, anger, frustration, loneliness, confusion, and hopelessness are issues that affect all of us on some level. When we lay our lives down to follow Christ, we experience peace, contentment, joy, thankfulness, friendship, purpose, and hope. It is because of our new relationship with Jesus that we have the ability to minister to others. We learned in the Self-Government Life Truth that we are to be witnesses. Hospitality is a great way to witness to others.

Hospitality originates in our homes. However, the spirit of hospitality needs to be with us always. We need to be ready to minister to others wherever we go. We need to be like the Good Samaritan who helped the wounded man beside the road. If we see someone in need, then we should help. We must not think that someone else will help them or that they've probably already called someone for help. We need to stop and minister to anyone that God brings across our path. At times, these needy people are tests from the Lord to see if we have a hospitable spirit. The writer of Hebrews says in *Hebrews 13:2*

(NIV) [2] *Do not forget to entertain strangers, for by so doing some people have entertained angels without knowing it.* The stranger who needs a meal, a place to stay, or has a flat tire on the side of the road may be God's way of testing our faithfulness. The stranger might just be an angel sent by God to see what we will do.

What should we do in our homes as we offer hospitality?

1. Be aware of people's needs.

We must love people and minister to them based upon **their** needs. It is important to remember that your gift or talent may not be what they need. You may have the talent to bake wonderful desserts, but what if they are diabetic? Have you blessed them?

One of the goals of hospitality is to meet the needs of others. We need to recognize their needs and seek to serve them. If they need a place to stay, give them a room. If they need food, feed them. If they need a listening ear, listen and hear them. If they need clothes, clothe them. If they need money, provide for them the best you can. As we learned in our last Life Truth, we are to excel in the grace of giving. God has given us an abundance and we are to share it with those in need.

When Jesus noticed that the crowds were getting hungry, He did not send them away. In fact, He told

His disciples to feed them. Jesus also told Peter to feed His sheep. He told him to do this three times; the same number of times that Peter had denied Jesus at the end of the gospel of John. Feed God's sheep. This phrase means meet the needs of the people. If they have physical needs; meet them. If they have spiritual needs (and we all do); meet them.

There are people all around us who are worse off than we are. They are in need. They are hurting. They need us to minister to them. As we have already learned, we are the ministers of reconciliation. We are to go out and share God's love with others. Do you know someone going through a hard time? Do you know someone in financial trouble? Do you know someone who is grieving over a loss? Meet their needs. Invite them over to minister to them.

God has called us to offer hospitality. Don't be afraid to do what God has commanded. Don't be nervous or fearful of how you should help. God will show you the way. We had a family over for dinner, and the chicken I grilled was so dry, we couldn't eat it. We just laughed, made something else, and had a wonderful time.

Don't be so busy with your own life that you don't have time to minister to others. God has not called us to be involved in the extracurricular activities of our society, but He has called us to offer hospitality.

If we are too busy to offer hospitality, then we need to get our lives in order and obey God.

Some think that offering hospitality is just inviting friends over to have a good time. While this is part of hospitality, it is not the intent. The intent is to minister to those in need. Look at what Jesus said in *Luke 14:12-14 (NIV)* [12] *Then Jesus said to his host, "When you give a luncheon or dinner, do not invite your friends, your brothers or relatives, or your rich neighbors; if you do, they may invite you back and so you will be repaid.* [13] *But when you give a banquet, invite the poor, the crippled, the lame, the blind.* Jesus teaches us that we need to be meeting the needs of people and not just having our friends over. Invite those who are struggling, hurting, and in desperate need of God's love. Look at what Jesus said about those who use their homes to minister in this way,* [14] *...you will be blessed. Although they cannot repay you, you will be repaid at the resurrection of the righteous."*

Don't worry about what you are going to say; just minister to others. Invite them over and listen to their story. Encourage them and point them to Jesus. When we are in need, a listening ear can be very healing. A meal can be very refreshing. How many of us have been going through a hard time and someone invited us over? Wasn't the fellowship refreshing? Didn't the care and concern from another give you some hope during your trial? Has anyone ever loaned you money or given you money when you were in need? Our goal is to mature to the point of being the lender, not the borrower in society.

2. Practice hospitality

Paul lists the different gifts that people have as he writes to the church in Romans Chapter 12: Some may have the gift of prophesy, encouraging, teaching, and perhaps giving. He lists a few more and then moves on to things we all must do starting in verse nine. He says in *Romans 12:13 (NIV)* [13] *Share with God's people who are in need. Practice hospitality.*
To practice is to perform. It means to carry out and do it habitually. Hospitality is a habit that we are to acquire. It is not just something we do once and then move on. You may read this chapter and decide to invite someone over. Don't think you've done your one hospitality deed for your lifetime. Hospitality is not a one-time event. It is a habit that needs to be practiced in the lives of Christians. We are to be using our homes as ministry centers. We are to help heal the many hurting people in our generation. Hospitality is tied to the command to go and make disciples. A great way to do discipleship is to invite someone to your home and share with them how to follow Christ.

As we see the needs, we are to practice hospitality. What would happen in our generation if all of the Christian homes began to minister to families around them? We would see a revival. We would see the gospel in action. One of the goals of the Life Truths is the multiplication of believers, and this multiplication is done when one family reaches out to another. All families have hurts, bitterness, anger, and lack of purpose. As we get our lives in order and begin to experience God's healing power, we need to minister alongside another hurting family and help them.

If we commit to making hospitality a regular part of our lives, we could see a revival across our country. By meeting people where they are, and then helping them to be healthy enough to help other families, we could see revival in our communities.
We have already mentioned the building blocks to a godly society. It begins with self, then family, then church, and then civil leaders. Look at the qualifications for a leader in the church. *I Timothy 3:1-2 (NIV)* *¹ Here is a trustworthy saying: If anyone sets his heart on being an overseer, he desires a noble task. ² Now the overseer must be above reproach, the husband of but one wife, temperate, self-controlled, respectable, **hospitable**, able to teach.* And in *Titus 1:7-8 (NIV)* *⁷ Since an overseer is entrusted with God's work, he must be blameless—not overbearing, not quick-tempered, not given to drunkenness, not violent, not pursuing dishonest gain. ⁸ Rather he must be **hospitable**, one who loves what is good, who is self-controlled, upright, holy and disciplined.*

If God wants to make sure that our leaders are being hospitable before we put them in positions of authority, you can be sure that he wants us to do it.

212

We must discipline ourselves to practice hospitality. We must remove our excuses as to why we are not having people over. We must obey the Scriptures and do it without grumbling.

3. Point them to Jesus

The main goal in hospitality is the salvation of a person's soul. While it is very important to meet people's needs, it will make very little difference on the Day of Judgment if they are cast into hell. The clothes, the meal, the cup of cold water, and place to stay, none of these things will matter in light of their eternity. We must minister and meet needs, but we must do it with the hope of them accepting Jesus and being saved from their sins.

Look at what Paul said in *I Corinthians 9:22-23 (NIV)* *[22] To the weak I became weak, to win the weak. I have become all things to all men so that by all possible means I might save some. [23] I do all this for the sake of the gospel, that I may share in its blessings.* We must point people to Jesus. If someone comes into your home and you minister to them, pray with them. Pray for them. If you are unsure as to how you can advise them based upon their trial, share your testimony about what God has done in your life and assure them that He can help them too.

Ask the individual or family if they would be willing to go through the Life Truths with you. Pass on the blessings of God's Word and use your home as a ministry center. This should be one of your main Life Truth goals. Acts reveals to us how Paul used the home he rented for a while. *Acts 28:30-31 (NIV)* *³⁰ For two whole years Paul stayed there in his own rented house and welcomed all who came to see him. ³¹ Boldly and without hindrance he preached the kingdom of God and taught about the Lord Jesus Christ.* Paul used his home for hospitality and for building God's kingdom.

Preparing your home to be a ministry center

If Jesus owned a home, how would He use it? If Jesus owned a home, what would He have in it? If Jesus owned a home, who would He invite over and why? If Jesus was coming to your home today, is there anything in it that you would be embarrassed to have?

If God has blessed you with a home, it is to be used as a ministry center. It is first to be used for your own family to worship and have communion with God. But then it is to be used to minister and to instruct others in the Word. You should view your home just as sacred as you would a church. If you would not expect something to be in a church, then it should not be in your home.

In order to use your home to its fullest potential there are a few things that need to be addressed:

1. Clean your house.

Yes, your home should be in order as we talked about in discipline, but it needs to be in order even beyond cleanliness. **Get rid of anything in your home that goes against God's standard of Holiness.**

There is a passage in Acts that reveals to us why the power of the Gospel is sometimes limited in our lives. *Acts 19:13-20 (NIV)* [13] *Some Jews who went around driving out evil spirits tried to invoke the name of the Lord Jesus over those who were demon-possessed. They would say, "In the name of Jesus, whom Paul preaches, I command you to come out."* [14] *Seven sons of Sceva, a Jewish chief priest, were doing this.* [15] *[One day] the evil spirit answered them, "Jesus I know, and I know about Paul, but who are you?"* [16] *Then the man who had the evil spirit jumped on them and overpowered them all. He gave them such a beating that they ran out of the house naked and bleeding.* [17] *When this became known to the Jews and Greeks living in Ephesus, they were all seized with fear, and the name of the Lord Jesus was held in high honor.* [18] *Many of those who believed now came and openly confessed their evil deeds.* [19] *A number who had practiced sorcery brought their scrolls together and burned them publicly. When they calculated the value of the scrolls, the total came to fifty thousand drachmas.* [20] ***In this way the word of the Lord spread widely and grew in power.***

Because of this incident, the people were seized with a holy fear. The Bible says that they came and openly confessed their evil deeds. God is real. There will be a judgment day. There is no need to hide your sin because one day it will be exposed. The Scriptures warn us that our sin will be found out. If our sin is not revealed here upon the earth, it will be revealed at the judgment seat.

People who are hiding sin do not want to use their homes as ministry centers. They are also not very qualified to be telling people that they can be free when they themselves are trapped in bondage. Be open about your sin and confess everything. Let Christ heal you so that you can minister to others.

The Bible goes on to say that many who practiced sorcery brought their scrolls together and burned them publicly. The Bible even tells us how much the items were worth (fifty thousand drachmas). A drachma was about a day's wages, so fifty thousand was a whole lot of money. Why does God reveal the cost? I believe he does this because he doesn't want us to worry about the cost when we burn or throw our stuff away.

We must get rid of the immoralities that go against the holy standard of God. Notice what the Bible says after they did all of this, *In this way the word of the Lord spread widely and grew in power*. "In this way" is referring to the people confessing their sins openly and getting rid of the immoral things in their homes. When we make our homes ministry centers that are purified from all of the evil influences in our society, it gives power to the gospel.

Here are some Biblical guidelines as to what types of things need to be removed from our homes:

1. God's name in vain - *Exodus 20:7 (NIV)* [7] *"You shall not misuse the name of the LORD your God, for the LORD will not hold anyone guiltless who misuses his name.* No one should be allowed to come into your home and take the Lord's name in vain. This means any books, magazines, songs, television shows etc… It must not be allowed in your home. There is a phrase that is in the church today that many say and even this is taking the Lord's name in vain. The phrase is, "Oh my _____."

2. Filthy Language - *Colossians 3:8 (NIV)* [8] *But now you must rid yourselves of all such things as these: anger, rage, malice, slander, and filthy language from your lips.* The Bible tells us to rid ourselves of these things and filthy language is one of them. Cursing should not be allowed in your home. Whether it is in book form or it comes by way of the television. It must be removed and the home kept in a Christ- centered state.

3. Witchcraft / Sorcery - Deuteronomy 18:10-11 (NIV) *[10] Let no one be found among you who sacrifices his son or daughter in the fire, who practices divination or sorcery, interprets omens, engages in witchcraft, [11] or casts spells, or who is a medium or spiritist or who consults the dead.* Christians should not be reading horoscopes, books about witchcraft, sorcery, or listening to anyone who says they consult with the dead. No matter if they make the witch "good" or they glorify such things. It must be abstained from. It is a deadly sin to allow such things into our homes.

4. Lewd Material - *1 Thessalonians 4:3-7 (NIV) [3] It is God's will that you should be sanctified: that you should avoid sexual immorality; [4] that each of you should learn to control his own body in a way that is holy and honorable, [5] not in passionate lust like the heathen, who do not know God; [6] and that in this matter no one should wrong his brother or take advantage of him. The Lord will punish men for all such sins, as we have already told you and warned you. [7] For God did not call us to be impure, but to live a holy life.* The sexual perversions are growing more and more in our generation and because of this the standard of purity has dropped in many Christian homes. There are magazines, books, movies, and television shows that depict sin as moral. In the last 50 years, immodesty has evolved to the wearing of almost nothing as being acceptable. Women are

commanded to be modest in their dress. The home should depict this. Men have enough issues with the sin of lustful eyes.

Some think very little about such sins and evils. Many think that getting rid of things is not necessary. They believe that we live under grace and it doesn't really matter if we have things in our homes that depict sin. This is a lie from Satan.

Look at what Moses said in *Deuteronomy 7:26 (NIV)* *26 Do not bring a detestable thing into your house or you, like it, will be set apart for destruction. Utterly abhor and detest it, for it is set apart for destruction.* Immoralities are teachings from Satan and we are to stand up for righteousness. If we are teaching people that they need to obey the commands of God, and then allow sin into our homes, we are hypocrites. We must maintain the standard of holiness in our homes.

John says in *2 John 1:7-11 (NIV)* *7 Many deceivers, who do not acknowledge Jesus Christ as coming in the flesh, have gone out into the world. Any such person is the deceiver and the antichrist. 8 Watch out that you do not lose what you have worked for, but that you may be rewarded fully. 9 Anyone who runs ahead and does not continue in the teaching of Christ does not have God; whoever continues in the teaching has both the Father and the Son. 10 If anyone comes to you and does not bring this teaching, do not take him into your house or welcome him. 11 Anyone who welcomes him shares in his wicked work.* We are told that if we allow such things into our homes, we share in their wicked work. We must purge the evil from our homes and make them holy unto the Lord. The blessings of ministry and the gospel spreading are dependent upon our obedience in this area. We are not to allow things in our homes that do not support the teachings of Christ.

2. Watch out for the yeast of hypocrisy

Our generation teaches us that we are to be tolerant. The Scriptures teach us that we are not to be tolerant of evil. We are not to tolerate it in our temples (bodies) or in our homes.
Proverbs 8:13 (NIV) *13 To fear the LORD is to hate evil;*

When we allow just a little evil into our homes, it mixes with everything, and begins to corrupt our relationships. We become more self-centered, more rebellious, and more angry. Our anger grows as we seek to be in control. Eventually, we lose our focus on serving others. Are you having issues in your home? Are you having issues with your spouse? Are your children being more rebellious? Perhaps, the root of the problem is what you have allowed into your home.

Evil influence is real. Too often, we do not take the dangers of it seriously enough. Do you remember what caused the church in Acts to be seized with fear? The demon possessed man turned to the seven sons and spoke to them. After he pointed out to them that they were not under the protection of

Christ, he beat them severely. The Bible says that if you are not in Christ, you are under the power of the evil one. *1 John 5:19 (NIV) [19] We know that we are children of God, and that the whole world is under the control of the evil one.*

Jesus warned the apostles to be aware of evil influences in their lives. *Matthew 16:11-12 (NIV) ...be on your guard against the yeast of the Pharisees and Sadducees." [12] Then they understood that he was not telling them to guard against the yeast used in bread, but against the teaching of the Pharisees and Sadducees.* The gospel of Luke tells us these teachings that Jesus is warning them about is hypocrisy. *Luke 12:1 (NIV) [1] Meanwhile, when a crowd of many thousands had gathered, so that they were trampling on one another, Jesus began to speak first to his disciples, saying: "Be on your guard against the yeast of the Pharisees, which is hypocrisy.*

If we are going to stand with Jesus on righteousness, then we need to be consistent. If using God's name in vain is sin, then we need to not allow it in our temples or homes. It is one thing to hear a lost person use God's name in vain in public and it is another for you to bring the sin into the home. If you have movies in your collection that use the Lord's name in vain, have cursing, sexual immorality, or any other evil that Scripture warns against, then you are bringing into your home the yeast of hypocrisy.

Look at this passage *I Corinthians 5:6-8 (NIV)* *6 Your boasting is not good. Don't you know that a little yeast works through the whole batch of dough? 7 Get rid of the old yeast that you may be a new batch without yeast—as you really are. For Christ, our Passover lamb, has been sacrificed. 8 Therefore let us keep the Festival, not with the old yeast, the yeast of malice and wickedness, but with bread without yeast, the bread of sincerity and truth.*

Get rid of the things that God calls sin. *Habakkuk 1:13 (NIV) 13 Your eyes are too pure to look on evil; you cannot tolerate wrong.*

Television is a powerful tool in the hands of Satan. Satan is using it to disciple many into the ways of sin and wickedness. Every year the shows get more and more depraved. As Christian parents, it is vital that we do not cause the little ones to sin. We are corrupt individuals, our flesh is strong and our sinful desires do not need to be fed. We must do all that we can to keep our homes Christ- centered. 2 John 1:10 says, *If anyone comes to you and does not bring this teaching, do not take him into your house or welcome him.*

When we have a television, we are allowing whatever they broadcast into our homes; from local channels, to cable, to satellite, and even the internet. We must guard our hearts and our homes from Satan's tricks that lead us and our children astray. Look at what Jesus said in *Luke 17:1-2 (NIV) 1 Jesus said to his disciples: "Things that cause people to sin are bound to*

222

come, but woe to that person through whom they come. *2 It would be better for him to be thrown into the sea with a millstone tied around his neck than for him to cause one of these little ones to sin.* An unguarded TV is saying, "Come in, Satan, and disciple my children." Disrespect, sexual immorality, cursing, taking of the Lord's name in vain, violence, lying and deception, greed, witchcraft, and mocking God, are all characteristic of what is broadcast today. Should we be allowing such things into our home? When your children are home alone what are they watching? Do they have access to shows that could trap them in sin?

What was it that caused the gospel to be stifled for a while in the book of Acts? It was the hypocrisy of God's people. When they openly confessed and cleaned out their homes, it gave power to the gospel. The Bible says, *20 **In this way** the word of the Lord spread widely and grew in power*.

3. Make your home a house of praise

Music is very powerful. We learned that we were created to praise God in an earlier Self-Government Life Truth. Satan loves to tempt us to sing songs or listen to music that does not glorify God. Music can get thoughts, beliefs, and emotions stirred. This is another vital area that needs to be guarded. It is a proven fact that certain types of music can cause us to become angry and rebellious. It can also cause us to be happy and excited. Certain types of music can

223

cause us to become lax in our morals, especially when it depicts immoralities as good and pleasing. Are you having issues of rebellion in your home? Find out what your children are listening to.

Look at this passage from *1 Samuel 16:23 (NIV)*
23 Whenever the spirit from God came upon Saul, David would take his harp and play. Then relief would come to Saul; he would feel better, and the evil spirit would leave him. The evil spirit would come and torment Saul. Saul would become angry, upset, and irritable. Saul would not let go of his pride and Satan would get a foothold in his life. He tormented Saul. Notice what would happen when David would play His godly music. The evil spirit would flee. When we listen to godly music in our homes, it drives the evil influences away. It is vital that we make our homes glorifying to God.

When people come into your home they should feel the presence of God. There should be no hypocrisy as to God's standards. There should be a peace in your home that only the Holy Spirit can bring as we make Jesus our Lord. Our families and our homes are to be examples of what it is to know Christ and walk in His ways.

No matter where you are on your journey with Christ, hospitality can start today. Have a hospitable spirit and be ready to minister to those that God brings across your path. Prepare your home today. Clean it out! Remove anything that goes against

God's standard. Begin praying about who the Lord wants you to minister to in your home. Make a plan to invite them over and begin the practice of hospitality.

WORKSHEET FOR FAMILY GOVERNMENT
LIFE TRUTH # 9
THE FAMILY IS RESPONSIBLE
TO PRACTICE HOSPITALITY

Question: How should Christians view their homes?
Answer: Christians should use their homes as ministry centers.

Romans 12:13 (NIV) [13] *Share with God's people who are in need. Practice hospitality.*

> Write out the Life Truth, question, and answer on one side of an index card and the verse on the other side. Keep it in your Bible for the week. Work on it every day individually and as a family. Have it memorized by next week.

According Romans 12:13 we are to
p_____ hospitality.
If we are to practice something does it mean that we just do it one time?

Hospitality is to become a habit in our lives.
Read 1 Peter 4:9. Why might someone grumble about offering hospitality?

Read Genesis 18:1-8. Abraham showed the men hospitality. What kinds of things did he do?
Did Abraham get out the left-overs or give the guests his best?

Read Job 31:32. What does Job say he did as a righteous man?

Would we be willing to do the same?
What might we need to do to make our home ready for a traveler?

Read 1 Timothy 5:9-10. To be on the church's list of widows meant that the church would support them.
H _____ was one of the qualifications for being put on the list.

Read Hebrews 13:2. The word entertain could also be translated to show hospitality. Why might God send an angel for us to show hospitality to?

Read Deuteronomy 23:3-6. Part of the judgment on the Ammonites and Moabites was due to their lack of hospitality. In verse 4, what did they not do?

Read 3 John 9,10. What were the four sins of Diotrephes?
1.
2.
3.
4.

Read Luke 10:8-12. What sin did they commit that caused such a judgment upon them? They rejected the teachings of Jesus. And they were not
H_____.

Read Matthew 25:31-40. Who are we really serving when we practice hospitality?

Based on this LIFE TRUTH what does your family need to do to get into the habit of practicing hospitality? Who do you know that is in need that you could offer hospitality to?

FAMILY GOVERNMENT
LIFE TRUTH # 10
THE FAMILY IS RESPONSIBLE
FOR HEALTHCARE

Jesus has called us to be the *salt of the world.* We can be *the salt* by showing the world the goodness of God through how we live our lives. Salt brings flavor to tasteless food. It says in *Job 6:6 (NIV)* *[6] Is tasteless food eaten without salt?* A Biblical Christian is one who is respected and considered wise. Look at what the Bible says will happen when we are following God's ways carefully: *Deuteronomy 4:5-7 (NIV)* *[5] See, I have taught you decrees and laws as the LORD my God commanded me, so that you may follow them in the land you are entering to take possession of it. [6] Observe them carefully, for this will show your wisdom and understanding to the nations, who will hear about all these decrees and say, "Surely this great nation is a wise and understanding people." [7] What other nation is so great as to have their gods near them the way the LORD our God is near us whenever we pray to him?*

Salt is a preservative. To preserve something is to keep it safe from harm and destruction. Salt is also helpful in slowing the process of decay. Jesus has called us to preserve our generation from moral decay. Think about the world today. If we are honest with ourselves, we have not been productive salt. God has called us to be ministers to our generation. He has called the family and the church to be responsible for the healthcare in our society. The word healthcare means an organized provision of care to needy people in our community.

The jurisdiction for healthcare is the responsibility of the family and the church. It is not the jurisdiction of the civil government. This doesn't mean that hospitals and other types of healthcare establishments should not exist. If God leads individuals, families, and/or churches to come together to form a hospital or private-care facility to meet the needs of certain individuals, it would certainly be within their jurisdiction. We have already seen this in our nation as many hospitals have been established by churches. Healthcare is more than just the insurance or the buildings that minister to the needs of people. It is God's way for Christians to rise up and meet the needs of hurting individuals, especially immediate family members. Christians are to care for those in their communities. They are to meet the health needs of the people around them. <u>To be healthy is to be sound in body, mind, and spirit</u>. John prayed for the good health of others, *3 John 1:2 (NIV)* *² Dear friend, I pray that you may enjoy good health and that all may go well with you, even as your soul is getting along well.* John not only prayed for the healthcare of others but he instructed us to meet the needs of those who are hurting and struggling.

I John 3:16-18 (NIV) *¹⁶ This is how we know what love is: Jesus Christ laid down his life for us. And we ought to lay down our lives for our brothers. ¹⁷ If anyone has*

material possessions and sees his brother in need but has no pity on him, how can the love of God be in him?
[18] *Dear children, let us not love with words or tongue but with actions and in truth.*

When we begin to meet the needs of the hurting around us, we are fulfilling our jurisdictional responsibilities in family government. This is just one of the ways that God uses His people to bless a nation and to reveal His love to the world.

We have been learning in family government that we need to handle our finances the way God instructed us to do. The excess that the Lord blesses us with (income beyond meeting our needs) is not just for our use. It is to be used to minister to the needs of others. This excess can be tied into healthcare. Our homes are to be His ministry centers. They can also be tied into healthcare.

God does not expect all of us to be doctors, but He does expect us to minister to the needs of others. We might be able to minister by paying someone's bills when they are sick. Perhaps we could minister by doing maintenance at someone's house when they have a need. This could be working in their yard or repairing something around their home. Meeting the needs of others means meeting their daily necessities, not helping them live in luxury. We are to use our available resources to minister to the needs of people around us.

Paul told Timothy in 1 Timothy 5:23 (NIV) to *stop drinking only water, and use a little wine because of your stomach and your frequent illnesses.*

In a Self-Government Life Truth, we learned that we are to live productive lives. *Titus 3:14 (NIV)* *14 Our people must learn to* **devote themselves to doing what is good, in order that they may provide for daily necessities and not live unproductive lives.** To provide for our needs and the needs of those around us is living a Biblically productive life. To be dependent upon anyone, when we are able to work, is to disobey God's command to work.

1 Thessalonians 4:11-12 (NIV) *11 Make it your ambition to lead a quiet life, to mind your own business and* **to work with your hands,** *just as we told you,* *12 so that your daily life may win the respect of outsiders and* **so that you will not be dependent on anybody.**

Remember, we are not to be dependent upon anyone. We've been told to earn the bread that we eat. *2 Thessalonians 3:11-12 (NIV)* *11 We hear that some among you are idle. They are not busy; they are busybodies.* *12 Such people we command and urge in the Lord Jesus Christ to settle down and* **earn the bread they eat.**

Welfare is giving aid or necessities to those in need. It is not Biblical for the civil government to handle welfare issues. This is outside of their jurisdiction. As we learned in the Self-Government Life Truth #10 - 1

Am Created to Work, it is the family and the church that is responsible to meet those needs.

Healthcare is the meeting of needs in a person's life physically, mentally, and spiritually. The Bible tells us that we are to physically give a drink to the thirsty and clothe the naked. We can help those with mental needs by offering an encouraging word, a listening ear, or giving them our time during difficult trials like death, divorce, murder, and other such tragedies. Spiritual needs in people begin with the basic need of salvation, but also include the need of Biblical instruction to avoid mistakes and to cope with the issues of life. The bottom line is that if someone we know is in need, and we are able, then we are commanded by God to meet their needs.

God's welfare design has a wide range of ways to help meet people's needs. Teaching people how to bless those who persecute them can be very healing. It will not only improve their spiritual health but will also strengthen their relationships. Teaching people how to truly forgive others will help them emotionally throughout the rest of their lives.

Why is the civil government not a good fit for the handling of welfare or a healthcare system?

Other than the obvious fact that they are not using the Scriptures as their guide, accountability is another reason.

There was a time when our families and churches handled the healthcare issues of this nation. They helped people and met their needs. However, families and churches dropped the ball and the needs of people began to grow. That is when the civil government stepped up to the plate. The plan seemed to be a good one at the time, but going against the Word of God is never productive.

We now have generations of people who have grown up on welfare. This has created a real problem in our society because there is no accountability in the system. It lacks a "good" plan that helps people become productive and fulfill their God-given responsibilities. As we learned in Biblical finances, we are to become the lenders and not the borrowers in society. If we are living on welfare, disability, or someone else's money, then we are not becoming the lender. This is not a productive life. The reality is that there will always be some who are unable to work and provide for themselves. God's design is for the family and the church to provide for them; not the civil government.

Way too many people in our society are on welfare when there is no need for them to be. They are mentally and physically able to work by the "sweat of their brow." Although they have the ability to be productive, they just want a handout. If they hurt-some or sweat-some, then they feel that they qualify for a disability. Remember, it was because of sin that God told us that work was going to hurt at times and that we would have to sweat in order to be productive.

This is what the Lord said to Adam after the fall. *Genesis 3:19 (NIV)[19] By the sweat of your brow you will eat your food until you return to the ground, since from it you were taken; for dust you are and to dust you will return.*"

How would accountability help the situation? The government is too far away from individual situations to truly help society. Our old natures are wired to be lazy and unproductive. We are sluggards by Adam's nature. If we can finagle a way to get someone else to provide for our needs, we will do it. People's needs must be met on an individual basis. There is no accountability when checks are mailed for everyone. It is not surprising that our sinful flesh wants to keep on receiving checks. But this is not God's plan for us. God's will is for us to become new creations and to learn to live productive lives. Suppose you had a family member who was in an accident and was unable to work. What would happen if you took them in, cared for their needs, and made them be accountable to you? The family budget would be negatively affected so you would have a big reason to keep them accountable. When they were healthy enough, you would encourage them to get back to work. Your accountability would get them back on their feet and help them to become productive in society once again. It is unlikely that you would allow them to sleep on your couch, eat your food, and spend your money while you went to work every day.

Unfortunately, many parents are allowing their children to grow up and do just this. We must keep people accountable as we work and provide for the needs of others. The health of our nation is dependent upon us to train others to live productive lives. We are not only to help people in need, but we are to teach them to obey all things that Christ taught.

Welfare, family services, and government assistance programs are not things the government is supposed to be involved with. When a tragedy strikes our nation, who do people look to for help? The government. Many people who have had their homes destroyed because of a "natural" disaster cry out to the government to build them new homes or a new town. This is not the responsibility of the government.

Families and churches are to meet the needs of people in times of tragedy. Communities are to look to God for help and come together to rebuild. The first questions that should be asked in a tragedy are: *"Lord, are you allowing this because we are out of your* will?" "Is this a test to see of our faithfulness?" In either case, we must turn to God and help one another. For us to be successful in the healthcare of our society, we must first take care of ourselves. There are three issues in America that are destroying our ability as families and churches to properly handle God's design for healthcare.

1. Debt

Debt is the first issue. We have discussed this in Family Government - Life Truth # 8. We cannot help others when we are enslaved in debt ourselves.

2. Amusement

The word amusement comes from two main words: "a" means *not*; "muse" means *to think.* So "amuse" means *not to think.* In hospitality, we mentioned the danger of allowing things that oppose the teachings of Christ in our homes. We are commanded in the Scriptures to remove such immoralities from our homes and lives. We are also commanded to be productive with our lives. Amusement causes us to go into a stupor and blinds us from the many needs right in front of us.

There are people hurting all around us while we are "busy" watching TV, going to the movies, playing video games, going to sporting events, and doing other "not thinking" entertainments to even care. These activities are distracting us from one of the main responsibilities in family government; the responsibility to meet the needs of others. We spend a ton of money on our luxuries, entertainments, and amusements. If we added up the amount of money each family spends on the latest "toys", the totals would astound us. These amusements numb us to the hurting world around us. We go into our homes, close our garage doors, and hide ourselves away. Jeremiah 48:10 (NIV) says, *A curse on him who is lax in doing the LORD'S work!* We have already looked at several passages that reveal to us our responsibilities in ministering in the matters of meeting people's needs. In Matthew, Chapter 25, we are told the righteous will feed the hungry, clothe the naked, help the sick, visit the prisoners, and give shelter to those in need.

The excess God gives us is not just for us. We are to use it to help others. What would be more productive in society? Playing *Angry Birds* and mastering all of the levels or walking alongside someone on government assistance to help them become productive in society? There are times in our lives for a little amusement, but we have a lot of work to do to get our nation back in order. We are the healthcare of society.

3. Gluttony

Moderation is a virtue. It is the avoidance of extremes. Gluttony is the extreme in eating. Gluttony is a sin. *Proverbs 28:7 (NIV)* [7] *He who keeps*

*the law is a discerning son, but a companion of gluttons
disgraces his father.*

The grace of God is what gives us self-control to not
be consumed by anything.
*Titus 2:11-12 (NIV) [11] For the grace of God that brings
salvation has appeared to all men. [12] It teaches us to say
"No" to ungodliness and worldly passions, and to live self-
controlled, upright and godly lives in this present age.*
God wants us to enjoy the beauties of His creation,
but He wants us to show restraint as well. There are
times to enjoy a nice meal with friends and family, but
if we are eating in excess most of the time, then it is
sin.

Many excesses that are condemned in Scripture
affect our ability to minister. When we overeat, we
are not taking care of our own health. Therefore, we
are less likely to meet the needs of others. *Proverbs
23:20-21 (NIV) [20] Do not join those who drink too much
wine or gorge themselves on meat, [21] for drunkards and
gluttons become poor, and drowsiness clothes them in
rags.*

Too often people make excuses for their eating
habits. The fact still remains that there are no
overweight people in countries that do not have an
excess of food. The real issue for us is the amount of
food that we are eating and our lack of daily exercise.

To be good ministers of the gospel, we must obey
the Scriptures, walk in self-control, and teach others

to do the same. When we overeat, we are more tired, have more health issues, and are less likely to minister to others. We are to take care of ourselves because we are the temple of the Holy Spirit. We do not want our God to live in a rundown temple. We want Him to be honored and live in a residence that brings glory to His name.

It is one thing to have health issues. It is another thing to cause health issues with our own decisions to sin. Sex outside of marriage brings us health issues. Drunkenness brings us health issues. Gluttony brings us health issues. We must see all these sins as serious hindrances to being servants of God. We do not have to look like Hollywood's version of health, but we do need to have a healthy diet and exercise program. We know it is wrong when we eat in excess. The prophet Amos condemned the nation for being self-indulgent and lazy. *Amos 6:4-6 (NIV) [4] You lie on beds inlaid with ivory and lounge on your couches. You dine on choice lambs and fattened calves. [5] You strum away on your harps like David and improvise on musical instruments. [6] You drink wine by the bowlful and use the finest lotions, but you do not grieve over the ruin of Joseph.*

As Americans, we have become lazy. We are not concerned over the ruin of our nation. James condemned such actions and worldliness. It says in James 5:5 (NIV) *[5] You have lived on earth in luxury and self-indulgence. You have fattened yourselves in the day of slaughter.* This is a warning to our nation as well.

FOCUS ON THE HEALTH OF OUR NATION

Jesus was called a glutton and a drunkard. He was called that because He was ministering to the hurting in society. He met their needs. *Matthew 11:18-19 (NIV)* *¹⁸ For John came neither eating nor drinking, and they say, 'He has a demon.' ¹⁹ The Son of Man came eating and drinking, and they say, 'Here is a glutton and a drunkard, a friend of tax collectors and "sinners."' But wisdom is proved right by her actions."* Jesus was called a drunkard and a glutton because he spent time with the needy. He was an example of righteousness. We are to follow His example.

Jesus helped the poor and the needy. Jesus came to minister to the sick. He taught people to be productive in society.

Look at this passage. *Mark 2:15-17 (NIV) ¹⁵ While Jesus was having dinner at Levi's house, many tax collectors and "sinners" were eating with him and his disciples, for there were many who followed him. ¹⁶ When the teachers of the law who were Pharisees saw him eating with the "sinners" and tax collectors, they asked his disciples: "Why does he eat with tax collectors and 'sinners'?" ¹⁷ On hearing this, Jesus said to them, "It is not the healthy who need a doctor, but the sick. I have not come to call the righteous, but sinners."*

Who are we spending time with? Is our focus to help the poor and the needy?

241

Is our focus to meet the healthcare needs in our communities?

When Paul was saved, the Lord gave him a vision to go and preach to the Gentiles. He met with the Apostles to make sure that he was hearing God correctly. The Apostles commended Paul and his work and said in *Galatians 2:10 (NIV)* *[10] All they asked was that we should continue to remember the poor, the very thing I was eager to do.* They told Paul how awesome it was that God had called him to reach the Gentiles, but that he must always remember to care for the poor.

In a sense, we are all unhealthy and in need of our sins to be forgiven. Jesus's message is for all, the rich and the poor alike. Many times the rich, however, do not believe that they need salvation. In fact, the rich often look down on the poor and the needy. They refuse to spend time with those who are dealing with hardships and issues brought on by bad choices. The Bible says that **Jesus touched the leper, he spoke to the outcast Samaritan woman, he did not throw a stone at the adulteress, and he ate with tax collectors and sinners.**

James tells us the kind of religion that God accepts. It says in *James 1:27 (NIV)* *[27] Religion that God our Father accepts as pure and faultless is this: to look after orphans and widows in their distress and to keep oneself from being polluted by the world.*

The word orphan comes from a Hebrew root word meaning "to be alone" or "bereaved". It is many times translated "fatherless." The idea describes a person who is without legal standing and is in need of someone to provide for them. In older generations, if you did not have a father in the home to provide for your daily necessities, you were unprotected in the community. (Baker Encyclopedia)

In our society, we have many children in the state's foster care system. These children are in need of people to provide for them. They have been removed from families who have neglected their needs. These children are oppressed and in need of help. Their parents are in need of love, forgiveness, and instruction. **Our godless government cannot help them like we can. We have the answer. We have the Healer. We have the Way, the Truth, and the Life to share with them! If Christian families would begin changing one family at a time, imagine what our society would be like in a generation? But If we continue to allow the government to handle this situation, we are a people headed for destruction.**

God expects us to look after orphans and widows. He is going to judge us one day on how we took care of them. I am a foster parent. I have heard it said so many times, *"I could never do what you do."* Many say, *"It would be so hard to help the kids and then give them back."* We do not do this because it is easy or because we like to make life difficult for ourselves. We do it because God expects us to. These children have their souls in the balance of heaven and hell. Most of them are not being brought up in Christian homes. They are not learning about Jesus and His teachings. Many are fatherless children in need of care and concern. We have an opportunity to sow the Word into these children and try to help the parents get their lives right with the Lord as well. God does not call us to live an easy life. He calls us to pick up our cross and follow Him.

Would Jesus help the orphans? Would Jesus help the widows? The Division of Family Services began in our nation when the church and its families decided to no longer help the "fatherless." We need to reach out to children in need and help them just as God reached out to us and helped us. It is better to have sown a little seed in a child's life than to have sown no seed at all. If families would rise up and fulfill their Biblical responsibilities, we would begin to see a greater harvest in future generations. But if we continue to sit back and let the government take control of this situation, then the harvest will be few and our society will become more and more immoral.

Is there a widow in your neighborhood that you could minister to? Is there an organization that you could join to begin helping orphans and children in need? If we are too busy to help the orphans and the widows, then we better remove some of our amusements and begin obeying God's Word. **Christian families and churches are responsible for the healthcare of our nation. The health of our nation is dependent upon our obedience to God and His Word.**

1. Obedience to God brings health

When we trust and obey the Lord it brings health. *Proverbs 3:5-8 (NIV)* [5] *Trust in the LORD with all your heart and lean not on your own understanding;* [6] *in all your ways acknowledge him, and he will make your paths straight.* [7] *Do not be wise in your own eyes; fear the LORD and shun evil.* [8] **This will bring health to your body and nourishment to your bones.**

Proverbs 4:20-22 (NIV) [20] *My son, pay attention to what I say; listen closely to my words.*
[21] *Do not let them out of your sight, keep them within your heart;* [22] *for they are life to those who find them and health to a man's whole body.*

When we praise the Lord it brings health. *Psalm 103:1-5 (NIV)* [1] *Praise the LORD, O my soul; all my inmost being, praise his holy name.* [2] *Praise the LORD, O my soul, and forget not all his benefits–* [3] **who forgives all your sins and heals all your diseases,** [4] *who redeems your life from the pit and crowns you with love and compassion,* [5] *who satisfies your desires with good things* **so that your youth is renewed like the**

eagle's. Praising the Lord is the "fountain of youth" that people are looking for.

Disobeying God brings health issues and diseases. *Deuteronomy 28:20-24 (NIV)* ²⁰ *The LORD will send on you curses, confusion and rebuke in everything you put your hand to, until you are destroyed and come to sudden ruin because of the evil you have done in forsaking him.* ²¹ *The LORD will plague you with diseases until he has destroyed you from the land you are entering to possess.* ²² *The LORD will strike you with wasting disease, with fever and inflammation, with scorching heat and drought, with blight and mildew, which will plague you until you perish.* ²³ *The sky over your head will be bronze, the ground beneath you iron.* ²⁴ *The LORD will turn the rain of your country into dust and powder; it will come down from the skies until you are destroyed.*

Walking in obedience to God is a protection from disease. *Deuteronomy 7:14-15 (NIV)* ¹⁴ *You will be blessed more than any other people; none of your men or women will be childless, nor any of your livestock without young.* ¹⁵ *The LORD will keep you free from every disease. He will not inflict on you the horrible diseases you knew in Egypt, but he will inflict them on all who hate you.*

When we begin to heed the discipline of God and repent, then God will begin to restore the health of our nation. We need to do our part by keeping ourselves away from the pollution of this world, by ministering in Jesus's name, and by following the

example that Jesus set for us. Look at this passage in *Hebrews 12:10-13 (NIV)* *¹⁰ Our fathers disciplined us for a little while as they thought best; but God disciplines us for our good, that we may share in his holiness. ¹¹ No discipline seems pleasant at the time, but painful. Later on, however, it produces a harvest of righteousness and peace for those who have been trained by it.*
¹² Therefore, strengthen your feeble arms and weak knees. ¹³ "Make level paths for your feet," so that the lame may not be disabled, but rather healed.

The power of the Gospel is dependent upon our obedience to God's commands. As we make level paths for ourselves, healing begins to flow. Level paths symbolize the narrow way of righteousness and holiness. We must walk as Jesus did. If we are going to see the lame healed and our society turned around, we must repent and make level paths for ourselves. We must get out of debt, stop wasting money on amusements, and stop being gluttonous. We need to be ready to share with those in need. This is God's design. Just like we learned in finances, *"He who gathered much did not have too much and he who gathered little did not have too little."* God said this to see if we would be willing to meet the needs of others.

2. Ministering in Jesus Name brings health

Disciples are commanded to go and heal. We most definitely need to ask Jesus to heal the sick, but sometimes the sickness or trials remain. When this happens, God expects us to be ready to serve. However, our own immediate family's needs must come first. Look at what Paul told Timothy about providing for family members who are in need. *1 Timothy 5:8 (NIV) ⁸ If anyone does not provide for his relatives, and especially for his immediate family, he has denied the faith and is worse than an unbeliever.*

If our family is taken care of then we are to go to those around us and see how we can help them. *Psalm 82:3 (NIV) ³ Defend the cause of the weak and fatherless; maintain the rights of the poor and oppressed.*

The nation of Israel, during the time of the prophet Isaiah, looked a lot like we do today. Listen to what the prophet told them in *Isaiah 58:1-14 (NIV) ¹ "Shout it aloud, do not hold back. Raise your voice like a trumpet. Declare to my people their rebellion and to the house of Jacob their sins. ² For day after day they seek me out; they seem eager to know my ways, as if they were a nation that does what is right and has not forsaken the commands of its God. They ask me for just decisions and seem eager for God to come near them. ³ 'Why have we fasted,' they say, 'and you have not seen it? Why have we humbled ourselves, and you have not noticed?' "Yet on the day of your fasting, you do as you please and exploit all your workers. ⁴ Your fasting ends in quarreling and strife, and in striking each other with wicked fists. You cannot fast as you do today and expect your voice to be heard on high. ⁵ Is this the kind of fast I have chosen, only a day for a man to humble himself? Is it only for bowing one's head like a reed and for lying on sackcloth* and ashes? Is that what you call a fast, a day acceptable to the LORD? ⁶ **"Is not this the kind of fasting I have chosen: to loose the chains of injustice and untie the cords of the yoke, to set the oppressed free and break every yoke?** ⁷ **Is it not to share your food with the hungry and to provide the poor wanderer with shelter-- when you see the naked, to clothe him, and not to turn away from your own flesh and blood?** ⁸ <u>Then</u> *your light will break forth like the dawn, and your* **<u>healing</u>** <u>will quickly appear;</u> **then** *your righteousness will go before you, and the glory of the LORD will be your rear guard.* ⁹ **Then** *you will call, and the LORD will answer; you will cry for help, and he will say: Here am I. "If you do away with the yoke of oppression, with the pointing finger and malicious talk,* ¹⁰ *and if you spend yourselves in behalf of the hungry and satisfy the needs of the oppressed, then your light will rise in the darkness, and your night will become like the noonday.* ¹¹ *The LORD will guide you always; he will satisfy your needs in a sun-scorched land and will strengthen your frame. You will be like a well-watered garden, like a spring whose waters never fail.* ¹² *Your people will rebuild the ancient ruins and will raise up the age-old foundations; you will be called Repairer of Broken Walls, Restorer of Streets with Dwellings.*

Did you notice the *thens* in these verses? For God to break forth and heal our land, we must fulfill our part by being the healthcare of society. We need to start taking care of the needy in our land and stop allowing the government to do it. We need the people of

God to fulfill the responsibility of being the healthcare system in our nation.

When Jesus sent out the disciples, part of their responsibility was to heal the sick. *Luke 10:8-9 (NIV)* *8 "When you enter a town and are welcomed, eat what is set before you. 9 Heal the sick who are there and tell them, 'The kingdom of God is near you.'*

When the church of Acts was being persecuted, part of their prayer was that God would heal people. *Acts 4:29-30 (NIV) 29 Now, Lord, consider their threats and enable your servants to speak your word with great boldness. 30 Stretch out your hand* **to heal** *and perform miraculous signs and wonders through the name of your holy servant Jesus."*

We are God's instruments of healing. We have a great responsibility to minister to those in our immediate family and to the needy in our communities. It is our job to provide for the needs of others and to minister to people as Jesus has ministered to us.

Look at what the apostle Paul said in *Acts 20:34-35 (NIV) 34 You yourselves know that these hands of mine have supplied my own needs and the needs of my companions. 35 In everything I did, I showed you that by this kind of hard work* **we must help the weak**, *remembering the words the Lord Jesus himself said: 'It is more blessed to give than to receive.'"*

Paul is not talking about putting a little money in the offering plate every once in a while. He actually worked hard to provide for the needs of his companions. This is the type of healthcare work that Christians and the church are responsible to do.

We are the givers and lenders to our communities. We are to meet the needs of the oppressed and provide the healthcare necessary to heal our land. We must walk alongside those in need and help them learn to lead productive lives in society.

Perhaps, you have a self-righteous pharisaical attitude. You believe that the poor are poor because of their own mistakes. It is by their own choices that they are drunkards, sluggards, addicts, and struggling in poverty. You would probably be right in your judgment most of the time. Most people are reaping what they have sown. But what would have happened to us if Jesus had not reached out to us? Without Christ we are wretched, pitiful, poor, blind, and naked. Thankfully, Jesus did not leave us in our sinful state. He became poor so that we could become rich.

Yes, they have made mistakes. Their lives are in a mess because of those mistakes. Yes, they are reaping what their actions deserve. But what a powerful opportunity we have to show them the love of God as we come alongside them and help them. It is not because they deserve it, but because of God's mercy that we go to them. We must love the world with the same mercy and grace that He has shown us. It is through this kind of love that we will see the unproductive in society become productive.

This will take hard work, sacrifice, and a working of the Holy Spirit in each of us. Our mission is to fulfill such a healthcare in society. When we stand before God one day, what will we have to show for our lives? Our list of the many amusements that we have participated in and acquired? The many levels of Angry Birds we have conquered? Or will we be able to say, *"I came alongside this family who was struggling and helped them become born again and productive in society."*

We can read a message like this and be very convicted. We can confess our sin and repent of it and God says, *"What sin?"* He remembers it no more. But God expects us to live differently. He expects us not to just hear the Word, but to apply it. He knows exactly what we need to do because we serve such an awesome God. *"Always remember the poor, be openhanded toward them, and walk as Jesus did."*

We must learn to live on less in order for us to share with those in need.

WORKSHEET FOR FAMILY GOVERNMENT
LIFE TRUTH #10
THE FAMILY IS RESPONSIBLE
FOR HEALTHCARE

Question: How should Christians view the needy?
Answer: Christians should provide for those in need, especially in their immediate family.

1 Timothy 5:8 (NIV) [8] If anyone does not provide for his relatives, and especially for his immediate family, he has denied the faith and is worse than an unbeliever.

> Write out the Life Truth, question, and answer on one side of an index card and the verse on the other side. Keep it in your Bible for the week. Work on it every day individually and as a family. Have it memorized by next week.

Healthcare is more than insurance and buildings that minister to the needs of people. It is God's will that Christians rise up and meet the needs of hurting individuals. It is our responsibility to care for those in our community and meet their health needs. To be healthy is to be sound in body, mind, and spirit.

Read 1 Timothy 5:3-16. To be on the "list of widows" meant that the church would provide for their needs. Verse four tells us who should provide for a widow. C_____ or
G_____ C_____.

In verse 8, who are we worse than if we do not provide for our immediate family members?
In verse 14, what are younger widows to do? Get M_____ and M_____ their H_____.

Based on this LIFE TRUTH what does your family need to do to get into the habit of practicing hospitality? Who do you know in need that you could offer hospitality to?

www.ingramcontent.com/pod-product-compliance
Lightning Source LLC
Chambersburg PA
CBHW061818040426
42447CB00012B/2713